Psychotherapy Series

Family Therapy
G.H. Zuk, Ph.D.

Brief Therapies
H.H. Barten, M.D.

Children and Their Parents in Brief Therapy
H.H. Barten, M.D. and S. Barten, Ph.D.

Psychotherapy and the Role of the Environment
H.M. Voth, M.D. and M.H. Orth, M.S.W.

Psychodrama: Theory and Therapy
I.A. Greenberg, Ph.D.

The Art of Empathy
K. Bullmer, Ed.D.

Basic Psychological Therapies: Comparative Effectiveness
A.J. Fix, Ph.D. and E.A. Haffke, M.D.

Emotional Flooding (Vol. 1 in New Directions in Psychotherapy Series)
P.T. Olsen, Ph.D.

The Initial Interview in Psychotherapy (Translated by H. Freud Bernays)
H. Argelander, M.D.

The Self-In-Process, Vol. 1: Narcissistic Life Styles
M. Nelson

A Publication of the National Institute for the Psychotherapies

EMOTIONAL FLOODING

VOLUME I IN THE SERIES
NEW DIRECTIONS IN PSYCHOTHERAPY
EDITED BY

PAUL OLSEN, Ph.D.

with

James Fosshage, Ph.D.
Kenneth A. Frank, Ph.D.
Henry Grayson, Ph.D.
Clemens A. Loew, Ph.D.
Henry Lowenheim, Ph.D.

HUMAN SCIENCES PRESS
72 Fifth Avenue,
New York, New York 10011

Library of Congress Catalog Number 74-12620

ISBN: 0-87705-239-5

Copyright © 1976 by Human Sciences Press,
72 Fifth Avenue, New York, New York 10011

Printed in the United States of America
6789 98765432

Library of Congress Cataloging in Publication Data
Main entry under title:

New directions in psychotherapy.

"Developed from the second annual professional conference and workshop of the National Institute for the Psychotherapies."
Bibliography: p.
CONTENTS: v. 1. Emotional flooding.
1. Psychotherapy—Congresses. I. Olsen, Paul. II. National Institute for the Psychotherapies.
[DNLM: 1. Emotions—Congresses. 2. Psychotherapy—Congresses. WM420 N277e]
RC480.N43   616.8'914   74–12620

CONTENTS

PREFACE

This book developed from the second annual professional conference and workshop of the National Institute for the Psychotherapies. The titles are identical: *Emotional Flooding.* The appropriateness of both the conference and this book, which is volume 1 of a projected series, *New Directions in Psychotherapy,* is self-evident. Directly stimulating emotion in patients is perhaps the most exciting and meaningful therapeutic trend that the mental health profession has witnessed in the past two decades.

Many of the chapters in this volume are based upon material presented at the conference. Others were written by invitation. All are original, prepared especially for this publication by the most prominent exponents of their "schools."

Particular acknowledgments are due not only to the zealous and loving work of the contributors, but to Ms. Betty Kent who worked heroically on every aspect of the manuscript; Dr. Sheldon Roen, who suggested the series; and to Ms. Norma Fox, who brought the conception to birth in a joyous labor.

CONTRIBUTORS

CHARLES W. ASHER, D. MIN., is a Jungian psychoanalyst and pastoral counselor who practices in New York City and Cresskill, N.J. A graduate of the C. G. Jung Institute for Analytical Psychology, he is director of counseling services, Tenafly Pastoral Counseling Center, Tenafly, N.J., and focuses primarily upon individual psychotherapy and marriage counseling.

JOHN M. BELLIS, M.D., is senior training therapist, Institute of Bioenergetic Analysis and supervising therapist, Connecticut Valley Hospital. He has a private practice in psychotherapy. He has published in the *American Journal of Clinical Hypnosis.*

MAGDA DENES-RADOMISLI, PH.D., is an existential-Gestalt therapist. She is associate clinical professor of psychology, Institute of Advanced Psychological Studies, and supervisor of psychotherapy, Postdoctoral Program of Psychotherapy, Adelphi University. She is also on the faculty of the New York Institute of Gestalt Therapy and the National Institute for the Psychotherapies.

MARGARET FRINGS KEYES, M.S.W., is adjunct professor of psychology, Lone Mountain College, and is also
affiliated with the Berkeley Center for Human Interaction.
She is the author of *The Inward Journey*. She trained with
Frederick S. Perls and Eric Berne and is engaged in the
private practice of individual and group psychotherapy.

MILTON V. KLINE, ED.D., is the executive director of
the Institute for Research in Hypnosis; director of the Mor-
ton Prince Clinic; and book review editor and editor emeri-
tus of the *International Journal of Clinical and Experimental
Hypnosis*.

DANIEL I. MAL'AMUD, PH.D., is on the faculty of the
William Alanson White Institute, New York University, and
the Workshop Institute of Living-Learning. Co-author of
*Toward Self-Understanding: Group Techniques in Self-Confronta-
tion*, he has also published in the *American Journal of Psychotherapy* and *Voices*. He has been in the private practice of
individual and group psychotherapy for over twenty years.

IDA P. ROLF, PH.D., is the originator of Structural Integration therapy ("Rolfing"), and a resident fellow at the
Esalen Institute.

SIDNEY ROSE, M.D., is N.Y.U. Fellow at the American
Academy of Psychoanalysis; a diplomate of the American
Board of Neurology and Psychiatry; and on the faculty of
the American Institute of Psychoanalysis. He is the former
director of group psychoanalysis at the Karen Horney
Clinic and a life member of the American Psychiatric Association.

JAMES M. SACKS, PH.D., is director of psychodrama,
Moreno Institute; co-ordinator of psychodrama, National
Institute for the Psychotherapies; adjunct associate profes-
sor, Brooklyn College (City University of New York); and

diplomate, American Board of Professional Psychology. He has published extensively in *Group Psychotherapy.*

THOMAS G. STAMPFL, PH.D., is professor of psychology and director of clinical training, University of Wisconsin. He is well known for his many publications and for the use of implosion in behavior therapy.

VAMIK D. VOLKAN, M.D., is professor of psychiatry and director of inpatient services at the University of Virginia Medical Center. He is on the faculty of the Washington (D.C.) Psychoanalytic Institute. He has published in the *Journal of the American Psychoanalytic Association,* the *Psychiatric Quarterly,* and other journals.

Dr. Volkan's co-authors are:

ANTHONY F. CILLUFFO, PH.D., currently in the private practice of psychotherapy in Edinboro, Pennsylvania, and

THOMAS L. SARVAY, JR., M.D., clinical assistant professor of psychiatry, University of Virginia Medical Center and in the private practice of psychotherapy.

chapter 1

INTRODUCTION

Paul Olsen, Ph.D.

While "emotional flooding" is a term aglow with an aura of newness, innovation, perhaps even chic, there is something venerable and almost reverential in the idea of directly stimulating affect in those people whom we now call patients. The concept is deeply rooted in religious belief and practice. Further, it has evolved in a largely consistent direction through a number of historical contexts: as a cure for physical and emotional afflictions; as a tool of exorcism; now as part of a technical armamentarium aimed at psychotherapy and consciousness-raising. The development of flooding techniques has been rather startling yet quite logical—its logic a reflection of how humankind has attempted to penetrate some of our tenacious age-old mysteries, which are apparently still perplexing, painful, frightening. The line of this development may at first glance seem circular; but as we shall see, we have not really arrived at the place from which we began.

In primitive societies—examples of which remain throughout the world—tribal physicians and shamans seem always to have associated both physical and mental disorders with intensely emotional properties. Indeed, many of their ritual cures were based on wild displays of emotion in which the patient, if he were not comatose or otherwise immobilized, participated fully, the major goal being to reintegrate him into his society (Kiev 1966). Such rites are still practiced in cultures such as the Haitian, where a last resort of the attempted cure of a refractory patient may involve roasting "over hot flames" (Kiev 1966, p. 172). Further, a variety of tribal afflictions may be easily identified with recognized modern-day syndromes, frequently depression or forms of schizophrenia (Kiev 1966).

As Henri Ellenberger (1970) points out, the shamans were primarily practitioners of psychosomatic medicine. Unfettered by the mind-body duality of Western philosophical thought, they quite naturally gave no consideration to the possibility of such a split. This is a vital point; implicit in the belief that any sort of illness contains emotional elements is an unverbalized acknowledgment of an unconscious process. It follows that liberation of these elements is a pathway to cure. In essence, the shamans were dealing with a crude but strikingly accurate concept of repression.

An obvious link between modern techniques and various forms of primitive cure is the emphasis upon working with the body itself, either by direct manipulation or via verbal instruction. An old concept, yet consistent—and lines might well be drawn even to such modern-day modalities as primal therapy and encounter and marathon groups that "facilitate change by producing excessive cortical excitation, emotional exhaustion, and states of reduced resistance or hypersuggestibility, which in turn increase the patient's chances of being converted to new points of view" (Kiev 1966, p. 174)—in short, that break defensive barriers directly, forcefully, and quickly.

Perhaps, with no shred of documentary evidence, we

may smugly state that far more cures were effected by bone-rattling witchdoctors than by Renaissance physicians who attempted to heal their lords with drafts of pulverized pearls and crushed gems. The Renaissance itself has produced a number of lingering misconceptions. Side by side with the flowering of its remarkable civilization existed the era of the great witch-hunts, an era which was not to ebb for at least two succeeding centuries. "Emotional flooding" remained in part a curative technique—exuberant dancing was still a treatment for tarantism in thirteenth-century Italy—but it gained prominent focus with persons afflicted by "demonic possession." Possession was truly a diagnostic category of its day, encompassing practically any form of religio-culturally determined psychopathology. Deviation from state law was treason, from church doctrine heresy; but the devil might be responsible for either.

Limiting ourselves to the area of mental illness, broadly defined, we can fairly claim that in Catholic countries before the middle of the eighteenth century, psychosis or markedly aberrant behavior was considered so bizarre, so beyond intellectual grasp, that etiology was frantically laid at the doorstep of the prince of darkness. This was especially the case when ravings, actions, or hallucinatory experiences contained elements of blasphemy or heresy. The primary issue in this context was the salvation of the soul, not the alleviation of an emotional disorder. Yet in accomplishing the former, the latter sort of fell into place —and in that sense the curative thrust was unspokenly, tacitly aimed at getting to a person's unconscious and unacceptable impulses and wishes. For example, while the ordinary ritual of confession is a classic purgative, many people who "confessed" under the duress of torture may well have been releasing repressed material. That is, they may not have been simply fabricating in order to avoid continued physical and emotional suffering; in all likelihood pain stimulated a flood of unconscious "crimes," such as murderous rage against authority figures, incest wishes, or any number of socially determined offenses.

The old exorcism rituals—a rekindled interest in which must be one of the strangest phenomena of the 1970s—were thus directed at rescuing the soul from Satan and returning it to God's grace. Their bonus effect might then be some relief of the body's anguish and sexual writhings, even if the body were broken on the rack. While exorcism in civilized times was largely a Christian, particularly Catholic, endeavor, the Jews also had their possessed brethren. The villain was a dybbuk which must be exorcized, and the curative attack upon the possessed person involved incantations, dancing, writhing, trembling—a kind of induced grand mal seizure. The usual result was fainting, hopefully followed by the dybbuk's departure.

The most prominent aspect of these religiously toned "flooding" techniques was the invocation of a higher power—the power of God, with the exorcist being a medium who might even act out the manifestations of a victim's affliction as he extracted the evil spirit and passed it on for God's disposition. (Shamans might do likewise but, depending upon tribal beliefs, many were regarded as having curative powers in and of themselves, thereby more closely resembling therapists.) In both Judaism and Christianity, the emphasis upon emotion persisted: to temper its expression or to liberate it in the service of driving evil forces from their human abode.

Thus the devil got his due. But in time he was regarded as a more secular symptom—except for his submergence into the ever-persisting occult underground and his later center-stage role in faith-healing sects. The person he possessed became diagnosed as demented and locked away under largely inhumane conditions. Less severe cases might perform skilled or unskilled labor for the state (Foucault 1965). And there the matter seemed to rest—at least for a while.

Real, scientific efforts at psychotherapeutics emerged in the nineteenth century, with the issue of emotion achieving prominence in the work of Charcot, and especially of Janet, one of whose immortal contributions was the finding that there is a tendency for an idea to emerge into action (Ellenberger 1970). With Janet the then most powerful tool of psychotherapy came full flower: hypnosis. The technique was aimed at inducing the patient to re-experience the full blast of repressed emotion suffusing some traumatic past event. Janet, however, was not only a hypnotist. Frequently he would actively engage a patient, talk with him, confront him, directly address the "sick" forces within him. Then he might attempt to contact the unconscious via hypnosis (Ellenberger 1970).

Tumultuous affect was stimulated by hypnotic techniques, but the major thrust of the method was an attack on the unconscious underpinnings of symptomatology. This approach was eventually labeled the cathartic method —catharsis not meaning simply the release of emotion per se. Actually "abreaction" was the term applied to the expression of affect, with the subsequent alleviation of symptoms being the "catharsis" (Rycroft 1968). Later Freud and his followers would eschew the so-called cathartic cure because it did not stimulate awareness of unconscious factors and hence did not result in insight—without which, in psychoanalytic thinking, there may be symptom substitution and, in effect, no cure at all. In contemporary terms, the cathartic cure might be described as a kind of behavior modification in which insight was not essential. For example, Breuer's original work with Anna O. was almost unbelievably meticulous, if not blatantly compulsive: under hypnosis he attempted to regress her, or bring her back, to literally every situation in which her symptoms appeared (Breuer and Freud 1955; Ellenberger 1970).

As psychoanalysis developed, hypnotic techniques and the cathartic cure were largely abandoned. The therapeutic approach achieved a cognitive or mentalist cast, with the expression of emotion primarily a by-product of the goal to make the unconscious conscious, to replace id with ego—an intellectual approach which, despite Freud's early pessimism, swept the bulk of American psychiatry into the psychoanalytic camp, while cathartic cure remained within the province of mental hospitals and supportive psychotherapy until the advent of psychopharmacology. Put in another way, unlike catharsis, dreams and associations led to the unrepression of memories, which might then stimulate connected emotional elements. This is the obverse of the trend that has developed in psychotherapeutic techniques over the past fifty years.

The figure at the center of this trend was Wilhelm Reich, one of the brightest stars in Freud's orbit, who was expelled from the orthodox psychoanalytic movement in the 1930s. Despite his unshakable belief in the orgone and its accumulators, his experiments in rain-making, his incredibly abusive *Listen, Little Man* (1970*b*), his identification with Christ, his conviction and imprisonment in a federal penitentiary and the approval of his sentencing by organized psychiatry and psychoanalysis, and the many supposedly authoritative testimonials to his paranoid schizophrenia, the impact of this man's ideas and techniques has been incalculable. There is almost no modern school of psychotherapy—including structural integration therapy, bioenergetic analysis, and primal therapy—in which the ghost of Reich has not materialized in some form. Gestalt therapy, too, frequently transforms a kind of Reichian character analysis into action, as does psychodrama. Even on the level of Reich's more "reputable" work in the first section of *Character Analysis* (1970*a*)—perhaps still the most brilliant exposition of applicable psychoanalytic thinking—the stronger interpretive assaults on a patient's character armor are obviously verbal techniques of emotional flooding.

But after the first section of *Character Analysis,* Reich ceased to be a psychoanalyst. And with that unintended defection, with his simultaneous banishment, were sown the seeds of a revolution. What Reich eventually did was to focus almost completely upon the body. Character armor became body armor—perhaps human armor, although he did not use that term. Wittingly or not, he sought to make the body-mind duality a seamless concept, believing finally that the body was the unconscious, not simply a reflection of it via mannerisms or posturing. Phrased with a slightly different emphasis,

> the armoring *is* the character structure in its physical form. Therefore if one can break down the armoring one will to the same degree change the neurotic character structure. But since the rigidity of the character is locked into the body, in the armoring, it is more effective to loosen the armoring than to try to change neurotic character traits by forms of talking-out therapy like psychoanalysis. [Mann 1973, p. 62]

Reich called attention to the visible bodily manifestations of character armor, such as muscular tension and rigidity. At root he is speaking of defenses; the body tightens or stiffens in certain areas in order to defend the person against the expression of unacceptable and threatening wishes, emotions, and impulses. Further, "all effective blocks to natural biological movements—e.g., of curiosity, play, sex, exploration, defiance of authority—where substitute actions fail to allow energy expressions, begin to build up armoring" (Mann 1973, p. 63). As each person lives with psychoanalytically defined defenses, so too is each person armored in the body. But whereas ego defenses are generally regarded as adaptive and necessary when not exaggerated to the level of symptomatology, Reich strongly imples that there is no benefit whatever in armoring—a position

with which most present-day therapists to some extent disagree. Perls (1969), for example, would quickly stop work
with a subject if he felt that potentially uncontrollable feeling might burst through the defensive structure.

Reich conceptualized and schematized armoring as
affecting the body in various segments, the most important
of which is the pelvic area. The eventual dissolution of
pelvic armor hopefully results in full genital sexuality,
Reich's sine qua non of the completely healthy human being. The method was called vegetotherapy (later orgone
therapy); and while the pelvis is the crucial region, armor
must first be dissolved "at the zone farthest from the pelvis" (Mann 1973, p. 64).

Here the parallel with the purely verbal character analysis is striking: the body is now the onion in need of systematic peeling from the outside in (Reich 1970a). As in
modern psychoanalysis, where the interpretive thrust is initially aimed at more intelligible defenses before reaching
unconscious material—the farthest points from the deep
psychodynamic target—so too does dissolution of armor
begin at the periphery. The pelvis, then, might be called
the last bastion of powerful defense, the freeing of which
leads to both emotional and physical cure. (The pelvis is
also considered to be the most vital bodily area in structural
integration; but its vitality is cast in a somewhat different
light.)

As noted, vegetotherapy employs a number of flooding techniques familiar to structural integration therapy,
bioenergetic analysis, and encounter methods—for example, shouting, touching, kicking, punching pillows, and specifically Reichian innovations of repeatedly opening the
eyes wide, grimacing, and repetitions of the gag reflex.
Reich regularly urged patients to disrobe in order to examine armored sections; then he might manipulate certain of
these areas—press, squeeze, or pinch them—which resulted in sharp expressions of anger (Mann 1973). Breathing techniques were also used to enhance relaxation.

Again, these techniques are no strangers to most present-day therapists even though they might not employ
them; but they were quite unique when Reich practiced
them, providing inexhaustable fodder for his critics well
before his use of orgone accumulators and other arcane
equipment. Further, these techniques must be rigidly separated from a number of provocative maneuvers used by
some therapists in efforts to elicit anger (or any other emotion)—for example, deliberately arriving late for sessions,
doing small "human" favors, raising fees at seemingly
inopportune moments. Such maneuvers are really ploys
and obviously not attempts to unrepress feelings by direct
work with the body.

Contemporary exponents of flooding techniques frequently maintain, whether or not they manipulate the body
—and most do not—that affect released in this way can lead
to actual character change and, in structural integration
therapy, to changes in the body itself. Personality alterations caused by periodic expressions of powerful feelings
is literally the backbone of primal therapy (Janov 1970).
Critics, however—and these remain in the traditional, primarily psychoanalytic camp—continue to emphasize that
such stimulation of emotion merely produces a cathartic
experience in the patient, without accompanying insight
and hence without lasting effect.

This position seems the result of unfamiliarity and, in
some cases, of blatant prejudice, for the modern stress
upon emotional flooding is extremely complex, as will be
abundantly clear in the chapters that follow. Here it is crucial to note that most exponents of the newer modalities
regard repressed affect not simply as an emotion or two
attached to a repressed traumatic event, memory, or perception; but that the entire range of potentially available
emotional responses is to some degree blunted. Thus a
person who does not experience powerful anger also does
not experience intense joy, and vice versa. The full gamut
is damaged and, for lack of a better term, repressed; every

facet is dimmed. Therapeutically, when one emotion floods through the rigidified character the potentiality for others to emerge is enhanced. The possibility of feeling fully is activated. To focus a person completely upon his emotions is held to cut projections, undermine denial—in effect to crumble the classical defensive structure. This unremitting focus is what gestaltists so often point to as the process of owning (or reowning) one's feelings.

Further, critics of flooding techniques appear largely unaware that the therapeutic process does not cease with the release of emotion. As the chapters in this volume amply show, newly expressed feeling is used to visualize, associate, interact, obtain feedback, and even to aid a purely verbal working through. A major objective is to focus as sharply as possible upon the experience of now, upon what is being felt now, in relation to oneself, the therapist, perhaps a group. Part of this work certainly involves clarification and even interpretation, although the emphasis upon the latter is not very strong. Yet repressed memories frequently accompany the emotional release, harmful patterns are perceived, and the past is linked to the present. In this sense, flooding techniques represent a far cry from the cathartic cure.

While these results occur rather regularly, there is still only a minor interest in traditional verbal techniques. And this underlines one of the most significant aspects of the newer modalities, drawing the historical lines ever tighter to Reich: there is a calculated semidisregard of intellectual and verbal material insofar as this is possible in a culture still so imbued with the mystique of communication through words. Feeling is primary; intellectual understanding is the by-product. The experince of being with someone is paramount; "good" conversation, table talk, is irrelevant.

Like the shamans, like the tribal physicians, therapists

in the mainstream of the modern modalities operate firmly within a broad segment of their cultural framework. Indeed, aside from the pioneering of Reich, they seem to have been created by the demand of the present young generation—a generation that has proclaimed in countless ways its mistrust of verbiage and attempted intellectual solutions to emotional problems. It is also a generation that has apparently cast itself into a kind of schizoid identity; namely, a hunger for emotional experience and a sense of personal authenticity. This hunger has shattered known, recent molds; yet what it has led to is a respectful resurrection of precisely that which is most primitive in all of us— our emotional lives. And the physicians of disordered emotions? With an armamentarium of incredibly sophisticated techniques, they, too, have nevertheless arrived at a starkly primitive therapeutic point of view: if the problem is with feeling, then one confronts feeling.

PART 1

Powerful emotion can often be released when patients are asked or trained to use their imaginations in creative visualizations, identifying with characters in their fantasy lives (and improvising dialogues among these characters), acting roles in interchanges with the therapist or with group members, or developing a threatening image in order to comprehend the repressed material behind the phobic symbol.

What appears to be a common thread in the following group of chapters is the technical emphasis upon this imagistic approach—an approach that largely requires the patient to assume profound responsibility for his own feelings and actions. In essence, he must reintegrate or repossess those aspects of his personality that he has repressed or split off to the detriment of a better-functioning self. He attempts this reintegration through a direct confrontation with feeling itself.

Chapter 2

EXISTENTIAL-GESTALT THERAPY

Magda Denes-Radomisli, Ph.D.

Gestalt Therapy at this moment of its development is primarily the legacy of a single man, Dr. Frederick S. Perls. Dr. Perls died recently; and it is the tragic irony of his fate that he died just at the time when he became ready to document his approach and to translate it into the more traditional, linear form of printed communication.

Prior to the year or two before his death, Perls's interests were centered largely on transmitting his method by example, through demonstration and teaching and treatment. As a result of this, there is no body of conceptualized knowledge to which one could refer as Gestalt theory. What there is of theory is a somewhat fragmented presentation by Perls and some other Gestalt therapists of various explanatory principles for the techniques of Gestalt therapy and for the attitudinal orientation of those involved with Gestalt therapy. These explanatory principles are rooted in the conglomerate and congruent influence of existentialism, academic Gestalt psychology, organismic theory as represented mostly by Kurt Goldstein, and psychoanalysis, particularly as interpreted in the early writings of Wilhelm Reich.

To my own mind, and as I practice it, Gestalt therapy is the direct, immediate, and authentic translation of existential theory into practice through techniques that fulfill and actualize the theory more completely than any of the other existential technical approaches currently in use.

Very briefly, existential analytic work is characterized by two distinguishing features. First, the particular nature of the analyst-patient relationship, which is, to use Buber's phrase, "a world where self is exposed to self." What is meant by that in more plebeian words is that the fullest possible presence is required of the analyst, as well as the willingness to confront reality both as it appears within him and as it appears in the relatedness between him and the patient; also the willingness and ability on the part of the analyst to fully encounter the patient and thereby to risk his own being. Further, to the extent that the patient's fragmented being-in-the-world prevents encounter, it is the analyst's task to confront the patient with this lack through his own presence and through the risking of his own grounded being.

"Encounter" refers to the full relationship that exists between two people as they are together in the world. It is always characterized by presence, which refers most broadly to the aliveness and alertness of a being. I shall return to the consideration of presence in a moment. Encounter is an extremely important concept in existential analytic thought as it is in Gestalt, since it is in the encounter of two people that each of the participants is altered. Encounter and transference are to be distinguished from each other in that encounter is always real whereas transference is always projected. Also, whereas some existential analysts see transference as a distorted aspect of encounter, others, such as Binswanger (1963), simply deny that transference exists at all. Medard Boss goes even further when he says:

> Transference is always a genuine relationship between the analysand and the analyst. In each being-together, the partners disclose themselves to each other as human beings; that is to say, each as basically the same kind of being as the other. No transfer of an affect from a former love object to a present-day partner are necessary for such disclosure, because it is of the primary nature of *Dasein* to disclose being, including human being. [1963, p. 123]

Rollo May (1961) regards transference as the distortion of encounter, which is included in encounter as one of its aspects, and he regards encounter as the totality of the relationship between patient and therapist, including even anticipatory thoughts of the session.

My own view is a little different. First, I disagree with May that encounter can exist in fantasy. The central characteristic of encounter, as I see it, is that it consists of a dialogical relatedness between two people. When intended dialogue lacks a partner, it becomes a monologue; thus one cannot speak of encounter in the absence of a real partner who is present in the real world and who participates in the encounter. Encounter always occurs in the Mitwelt ("with" world), so that by definition it implies the presence of another. Second, and as a corollary of my first point, one can speak of encounter between patient and therapist only after the patient in his full presence has been engaged by the therapist. In other words, regardless of how much presence, commitment, and intention toward encounter one member of the dyad possesses, if the other member is physically absent or is psychologically abstracted, diffused, uncommitted, unpresent, no encounter can occur. I see encounter, then, as an aspect of man's intentionality toward his world, and I regard as the first step in treatment the confrontation of the patient precisely with his specific techniques for dodging his potential for encounter.

Encounter, then, to my mind is not an existential given, but is rather a potential between people and for each person, which awaits a conscious intention, a courageous risking of one's sealed-off-ness for its actualization. To speak of encountering a poem or a painting as May does, for example, is to confuse the concept of encounter—which is always dialogical and diadic and takes place in the Mitwelt—with the concept of confrontation, which is unilateral, although it can take place either in the Mitwelt or in the Eigenwelt. Confrontation requires presence, but it does not require a partner. Thus, the sharpness of my perception of a painting will depend on the degree of my momentary presence (aliveness) as I confront it—or rather as I confront myself with it. The relatedness is unilateral, and it takes place in my Eigenwelt.

Similarly, the sharpness of my awareness that someone, say, is not listening to me, will depend again on the degree of my presence as I confront myself with the fact of his not listening (Eigenwelt). Now if I also confront him (Mitwelt) with this fact, I will have unilaterally confronted him with the potential for an encounter, but I will not have insured an encounter. Whether the encounter will take place or not depends on our mutual choices and not on my intention alone. It depends whether he will confront himself with my confrontation of him, since encounter requires the actualization of a dialogue of which the other, with his presence and his intent, is a member.

From this follows my third point, where I would regard transference not as one aspect of encounter but rather as one aspect of those forces operating in the patient or in the therapist that prevent the actualization of the encounter. This seems to me logical, given that encounter implies both the full accurate confrontation of the other being and the participation with the other being in reality, in the here and now; whereas transference implies a distortion of reality as it exists in the here and now in favor of a perseverative insistence on the past—on the not now. One cannot then regard distortion as part of accuracy; one must postulate it as that which prevents accuracy.

Since I have been speaking of presence all along, let me just clarify it here for a moment. It is by no means a mysterious entity, as it is sometimes taken to be by those unfamiliar with its use in existential thought. Most people know the concept in the form of "stage-presence" regarding an actor. In both usages, the concept refers to a full, alive, alert, nontruncated there-ness. It refers to being without hiding. In simple language one would say of a person who has presence that "he comes across." Put another way, presence is that quality of a person which reveals his who-ness with vibrant immediacy. It is characterized by courage because it involves the person's continuing affirmation of his being in the face of each new moment.

The second distinguishing feature of existential analytic work resides in what is regarded as the analytic task— namely, the phenomenological analysis of the patient's being-in-the-world and his participation and responsibility in the choice of this world. Or, as Sartre (1956) points out, existential analysis aims at objectifying the subjective components of the patient's life.

Now it is my contention, which I hope to demonstrate to you, that Gestalt techniques train people precisely in phenomenological observation, in the ability to acquire and sustain presence, and in the requisite contact[1] for meaningful encounter. As such, these techniques represent the most authentic available translation of existential theory into practice.

I should like, then, to give you a brief overall presenta-

---

1. Contact in Gestalt thought is considered the end product of receptor function operating in a state of health. To be in contact is the natural state of the awake, healthy human being. It requires awareness—the unfettered ability to perform figure/ground shifts. It is possible to block consciousness of contact where shifts in figure/ground do not occur, and instead of two differentiated parts of the field, there is an undifferentiated uniform field which is referred to as confluence and is regarded as an aspect of malfunction. Identification for example is an instance of confluence.

tion of some of the salient features of Gestalt therapeutic thought.

First, in any therapeutic approach, as you know, goals form a major guiding principle in both the content and, hopefully, the outcome of treatment. In Gestalt as well as in other existential approaches, the goal is not one of adjustment. In some ways, it is quite contrary.

Adjustment in psychotherapeutic work implies a molding of the individual until he fits the particular environment of which he is a part. It implies that one's own world and the general world must be juxtaposed and merged. Thus I am adjusted to traveling on the New York subway to the degree that I regard myself as an object to be jostled and shoved and not as a person entitled to some courtesy. Adjustment is a method of dealing with the general world by giving up portions of the self. I do not mean to say here that the person who is "healthy" in my sense cannot travel on the subway. He can, of course—but at a cost. The cost is his continuing consciousness that he is being mistreated and continuing guilt that he mistreats others. Notice then here the apparent contradiction: the fellow who is adjusted is not conscious of his discomfort, he does not have the "discomfort-symptom," he is willing to cut off his consciousness and to travel as object; the fellow, on the other hand, whom I call healthy, has the "discomfort-symptom." He has retained his consciousness of it, precisely because of his consciousness of his being.

Clearly, then, any analyst's preference in terms of goals in treatment will vary with the analyst's commitment regarding the value of one state as over the other. The behavior-modification therapists, for example, are deeply committed to adjustment as their goal, since it implies symptom freeness and smooth functioning within the society. Given that, their emphasis is strongly on technique and on the technical aspects of life, they teach their patients techniques of adjustment to the general world as it is.

The contrary is true in existential analysis. The goal of treatment is to enable the patient to fulfill his Dasein. It is to enable the patient to experience his existence as real, immediate, and authentic. To enable him to choose his being and his being-in-the-world and to commit himself responsibly to the fulfillment of his potentials. The emphasis is not on symptom freeness as such. As a matter of fact, since confronting the new and risky always involves anxiety, a person who is healthy in the existential sense may function with considerably more conscious anxiety than the adjusted person, also with more conscious guilt (May 1958). The adjustment view of the goal of treatment has a further implication; namely that if you try to adjust a person to the world as it is, overtly you are assuming that the world as it is, is fine; and tacitly you are discouraging change and innovation. The world, however, as it is, is not fine, and we all know it. Consequently adjusting to it is not fine either, because it involves curtailing consciousness, forfeiting being, surrendering existence. "Cure," then, in existential analysis, has to do with enlarging the person's existence and enabling him to authenticate it to the fullest possible extent.

The particular technique used in Gestalt therapy is the technique which Perls named "experiments." These experiments are based on the premise that there exists an autonomous criterion for organismic health, independent of cultural values or analogical models, rooted entirely in the organism's unfettered ability to form or destroy Gestalten.

Perls, extending the work of the academic Gestalt psychologists, applied the Gestalt principles of perception to the realms of motivation and motoric behavior. Thus, according to him, the phenomenal world of a person is always organized by his most pressing need, which becomes figure —until the need is satisfied and recedes into the background to give way to another organizing need. To the extent that the elasticity of the figure-ground formation is disturbed, we find malfunction. Experimentation in Gestalt therapy is aimed toward making the patient aware of his phenomenal world, both extroceptive and proprioceptive, and of the forces that move him to organize it into the particular Gestalt that he does at any given moment. Perls distinguishes three primary mechanisms that interfere with adequate Gestalt formation: retroflection, introjection, and projection. He regards these mechanisms of sufficient import that he tentatively suggests a classificatory schema of neurotic character types based on the predominance in the character structure of one of the three mechanisms (Perls, Hefferline, and Goodman 1951).

Retroflection means literally "to turn sharply back against." To quote Perls:

> When a person retroflects behavior, he does to himself what originally he did or tried to do to other persons or objects. He stops directing various energies outward in attempts to manipulate and bring about changes in the environment that will satisfy his needs; instead, he redirects activity inward and *substitutes himself in place of the environment* as the target of behavior. To the extent that he does this, he splits his personality into "doer" and "done to." [Perls, Hefferline, and Goodman 1951, p. 146]

Perls further contends that retroflective behavior is primarily motoric in that the unexpressed impulse is checked at the muscular level, where it appears as unaware chronic tension. Thus, for example, the unexpressed urge to be "biting" is retroflected in chronically clenched jaws. Or, as another example, repeated acts of clumsiness are often retroflected annoyance.

In the therapy session, the patient's attention is always called to retroflective behavior. The experiment is set up to allow him to fully experience the behavior, at first through exaggeration—if someone talks to me through clenched teeth, I will ask him to clench his teeth to the utmost possible extent of his ability, in order to get the feel of it, that is, in order that he sharply focus on the activity and thereby remove it, at least for the moment, from the category of habit. As the next step, I will ask him to reverse the retroflection, for example by making biting motions with his teeth, or allowing his teeth to chatter, or saying nasty things, or whatever else seems to organically grow out of his own awareness. The aim is to allow the patient to make his own both the retroflective act and the behavior it holds in check, and to find a new level of integration in which both parts can obtain overt conscious expression. If the patient is able to genuinely experience the retroflection and its reversal, some meaningful memory of fantasy will invariably emerge. This then becomes the next figure to which both the patient and I address ourselves.

The concept of introjection in Gestalt therapy corresponds exactly to the common clinical usage of that term. It refers to the grafting of some aspect of another onto the self-system. But whereas in traditional thought the function of introjection is seen as both defensive and adaptive, in Gestalt therapy it is always regarded as pathological. Perls analogizes the ingestion of food to the ingestion of environmental influence into the personality. He claims that only that ingested material, be it physical or spiritual food, that has assimilated through destruction and reconstruction is helpful. And that material which is swallowed whole, that is, introjected intact, becomes the source of neurosis or of an upset stomach. Carrying the analogy further, an analogy which he sees as a genuinely organic correspondence, Perls devised several experiments related to eating through which he hoped to contact the introjects in the psychic realm.

Although I agree with Perls in regarding introjection as a pathological process, and not as an adaptive one—in the sense that in an optimum environment a small child's interactions would be sufficiently freely grounded in safe reality that he would not need to introject—I do not find the eating experiments particularly helpful. I prefer, in my work, to listen to voice quality and syntax, to watch for gestures and postural characteristics, to attend to expressions of "I should" and "I must" and so on, and to devise experiments on the basis of these signs as aids in the uncovering of introjects.

As with introjection, the term "projection" is also used in the traditional sense in Gestalt therapy. It is used to mean the attribution of an aspect of the self onto another person.

In my estimation, Perls makes a major contribution here in his emphasis on what he refers to as the "it" language. He says that, typically, modern dissociated man has evolved a language to reflect his alienation from himself and his abdication of responsibility for himself by projecting through the language his own impulses, feelings, and bodily states onto the outside world:

> The prevention of outgoing motion and initiative, the social derogation of aggressive drives, and the epidemic disease of self-control and self-conquest have led to a language in which the self seldom does or expresses anything; instead, "it" happens. . . . In such a world of projections a man, instead of raging, is "possessed" by a temper. . . . Instead of thinking, a thought "occurs" to him. He is "haunted by" a problem. His troubles "worry" him. [Perls, Hefferline, and Goodman 1951, p. 215]

"It" language is always presumptive evidence of projection, since it involves the disowning of an aspect of the self and seeing it as a characteristic of the outside world. The impersonal mode such as, for example, "one might think," also belongs in this category, as does the common, "You feel bad when you are mean, you know," referring to one's self. In the latter case, the projection is extremely apparent, since it is directly contained in the language.

Further, it is not infrequent to hear patients complain while referring to their own bodies that "the head hurts" or "the arm is stiff" as a reflection of a fragmented sense of self, where the speaker projects his pain onto an alien head on his neck.

Experiments for the recovery of these projections center around a vigilant and assiduous awareness of their occurrence, and the conscientious recasting of every "it" into an "I" with the appropriate exploration as to why the "it" was necessary at the particular time.

What those experiments make clear is that the imparting of information to the patient in a Gestalt therapy session occurs minimally through interpretation and maximally through the disruption of habitual character modes. The patient is required to learn the phenomenological observation (that is, observation without premises) of his own functioning. The emphasis is on how and what rather than on why; it is on active participation rather than on a passive recipient state.

Awareness, then, is the key tool of Gestalt therapy. Awareness, directed inward, toward bodily and emotional states, permits the discovery of selfhood based on the actualities of personal existence. "Who am I?" becomes a matter of perception rather than conjecture. "Who am I?" becomes "How am I?" in the literal sense—"How am I breathing now?" "How do I contract my stomach muscles?" "How am I closing my ears to what is being said?" "How is the quality of my voice?" and so on.

As the observations become more vigilant and more accurate, areas of resistance readily appear. The common core of these resistances is as a rule the discrepancy between the felt awareness of the self and the habitual verbal conceptualizations about the self. The tension between these two polarities is the arena for every human being where the battle of authenticity is fought. Here too, is the arena where introjects are identified and worked through either into rejects or into genuinely assimilated aspects of the self.

Similarly, with increased accurate self-awareness, projections decline. Since one's who-ness is determined on the basis of actual experience, the casting onto others of this experience becomes less possible and less necessary. In this connection, Perls points out that the characteristic referred to as intuition in our society consists really of a person's projectionless awareness of others' verbally unexpressed intentional and/or unconscious attitudes toward him. Some implications that emanate from this emphasis on accurate—not objective, but accurate—self-perception, are as follows:

First, in Gestalt thought as in existential philosophy, identification and identity development are regarded as antagonistic processes. The former has to do with a sacrifice of autonomy for a measure of safety: the latter has to do with the continuing affirmation of one's awareness of self-experience as it presents itself and with the continuing risk of admitting into awareness new experiences of the self that may not fit with the old. This means, that identity, when it is experientially based, is not a fixed entity but rather a more or less fluid process in time. It is not established once and for all but is chosen and affirmed again and again in the light of the immediacy of actual experience.

Second, in both Gestalt and existential thought responsibility for authentic selfhood resides with the individual. Man chooses his being and within the limits of his freedom makes himself who he is. Consequently, identity is not a determined accident but a responsible choice in an active mode. A great deal of the experimentation of which I have spoken earlier is aimed precisely toward the mobilization of this active mode and toward the awareness of responsibility.

Take as an instance a simple experiment where a person is asked to say sentences all beginning "Here and now I am aware" and all ending "and I take responsibility for it." The experiment is so simple as to seem simpleminded. And yet, time and again I have witnessed in people sudden enlightening reversals regarding the active or passive role they play in their ordinary functioning. The sentence "I have a headache, and I take responsibility for it," when properly contemplated and perceived, gives rise to a context of selfhood totally different from that say of a sentence, "He gave me a headache by getting me angry."

It is at about this time that people as a rule start making notes to themselves to ask me in the question-and-answer period: "What about those tragic accidents of fate for which the individual is not responsible?" And the answer to that is that I am not that big a fool. I know that they exist. I know that there are grave limits to human power. (That was only half a pun.) But I am also convinced that within those limitations human beings do choose their being— and the more awarely they do so, the better off they are. Also, whether they are aware or not of the choice does not alter their responsibility for it.

The third implication of this emphasis on self-awareness has to do with a view of the individual's basic relatedness to the reality of his world.

In existential philosophy, self and world are said to stand in a dialectical relation to each other, where a curtailed self implies a reduced world. Conversely, I am suggesting, an expanded self implies an enriched world.

With increased self-awareness and decreased projections, receptor functions cease to be blocked and orientation to the world acquires experiential immediacy. In Gestalt therapy, this is referred to as the awareness continuum and is regarded as the understructure of accurate reality perceptions.

A final word, regarding what Gestalt therapy is not:

As many of you are probably aware, the techniques of Gestalt therapy have, in the recent past, been adopted by various cultural movements for the pursuit of activities that range in claim from the therapeutic to the entertaining.

What I earlier referred to as experiments have recently appeared in elaborate mutation as games (literally table games), cure-alls, keys to instant enlightenment, and the magic carpet to the Way. Gestalt therapy is none of these.

I would like to mention three[2] salient aspects among many in which Gestalt therapy differs, in terms of technique, from say sensitivity training with which it is, unfortunately, not infrequently confused. In terms of philosophy and its implications, the differences are so radical and so numerous that time does not permit me to deal with them here.

First, the techniques of Gestalt therapy do not generate experience but rather allow individuals to become aware of the experience they spontaneously generate.

Second, Gestalt therapy is not oriented toward catharsis in the pregnant instant but is rather firmly committed to the need of disciplined working through of malfunction in the context of a therapeutic dialogue of I and thou.

Third, Gestalt group work is not primarily oriented toward the improvement of specific interpersonal relations in the group setting. In other words, its emphasis is not on making it in terms of approval, love, et cetera, with the other group members. Rather the group is utilized to sharpen self-awareness in the context of the group, with emphasis on improved reality perceptions in relation to the group and of the freedom of choice to relate or not to individual group members.

It follows that the goals of Gestalt therapy also differ

2. I have made some of the following points in a previous article titled "Gestalt Group Therapy: Sense in Sensitivity."

radically from the goals of those movements that have adopted its techniques. The aim of existential Gestalt treatment as I see it is to help the single being become rooted in reality so that he may authenticate his individual existence and responsibly affirm the choice of his world and the choice of his unique sovereign self.

chapter 3

SHUT UP!
A PSYCHODRAMATIC TECHNIQUE
FOR RELEASING ANGER

James M. Sacks, Ph. D.

The reader unfamiliar with psychodramatic techniques will find the following glossary of terms useful.

Auxiliary ego: A therapist-actor, sometimes a member of the group, who assists in the drama by taking roles.

Director: The therapist.

Double: An auxiliary ego who takes the role of the protagonist, usually standing behind him. The double speaks the protagonist's unexpressed thoughts.

Protagonist: The person whose life is being explored psychodramatically.

Soliloquy: A speech by the protagonist (sometimes by his double) which is understood to be inaudible to the other actors in the drama.

Warm-up: The initial phase of the session, during which the group becomes ready for the drama.

INDICATIONS AND CONTRADICTIONS

Since it is known to be especially effective in facilitating catharsis of latent aggression, psychodrama is sometimes unfairly stigmatized as overemphasizing this element in psychotherapy. Indeed, the simplicity of the idea of mere ventilation of anger does seduce certain therapists into universalizing the scheme as a near total approach to treatment. While abreaction of anger may provide immediate gratifaction, it does not necessarily lead to any change in the intrapsychic dynamics that generate irrational anger. Nonselective stress on the discharge of anger in therapy may even discourage the development of reasonable controls or foster a spurious anger to please the therapist. It may also lend support to paranoid defenses and discourage self-understanding by externalizing blame. Notwithstanding these cautions, there are times when it is clear that a patient is in fact overinhibiting the experience of hostile emotion and that his dread of these latent urges generates symptoms. Anger-facilitating techniques such as the one about to be described would seem justified only when the therapist expects the emergence of anger to relieve rather than frighten the patient and when the experience may be utilized to expand insight. Goals of such procedures are:

1. To enable the patient to taste the sensation of his own anger in a safe setting where he can re-evaluate the actual need for evading this emotion.

2. To relieve symptoms based on the diversion of hostile energy into unwanted manifestations.

3. To provide access for the ego to these energetic feelings for sublimated uses. With an increased capacity to

experience anger consciously, the patient can often find self-fulfilling and socially useful ways to direct it.

4. To facilitate the process of emotional release. Once in contact with these feelings, the memory and habituating influence of the experience makes it easier to repeat than it was to accomplish the first time.

5. To encourage involvement in the process of self-exploration. This occurs by means of a live demonstration that potential emotions exist that had been unavailable to conscious experience and that there are ways to gain contact with them.

6. To provide preconditions for proceeding to further insight. For example, once a patient is fully aware of his anger, its intensity, and the situation that generated it, he is in a better position to acknowledge that the rage is transferential in nature, where the sensitivity toward this kind of situation originated, why it was inhibited, and so on.

Indications for the use of any hostility-enabling procedure should include evidence that the patient's symptoms actually are based on overcontrol of latent anger and that there is sufficient ego-strength to deal advantageously with this anger once it has emerged. The result must be integratable by the ego rather than traumatic to it.

To resist exaggerated expectations, it should be recalled that the release of bound anger, while sometimes helpful, does not automatically result in the disappearance of all symptoms based on the diversion of hostile energy. Neither catharsis nor insight is a panacea. The emotional habits of a lifetime develop a functional autonomy no longer dependent on their original cause. Abreaction facilitates but does not guarantee insight, just as insight facilitates but does not guarantee reduction of symptoms.

Introduction to the Technique

I once had the misfortune to try to teach a psycho-drama class in a room adjacent to a group working in a familiar encounter style. Through the wall a voice thun-dered, "I am angry," over and over, with occasional urg-ings by the leader to yell louder. Such an approach usually leads the reticent protagonist to further intimidation or to mechanical conformity without the experience of affect. In the technique to be described here, the attempt instead is to dam up whatever free aggression remains to the inhib-ited protagonist and to allow a sudden release with the timing controlled by the protagonist himself. The role of the auxiliary ego, paradoxically, is to suppress rather than to spur the protagonist on.

Another drawback in the "I am angry" approach is its abstract quality. People are rarely angry in general. Anger, like love, has an object, is triggered by concrete events, and calls out particular responses. Someone might be angry, for example, with her fiancé (object), because he procrastinates instead of working (initiating circumstance) and she wishes to quit her own job to punish him (mode of expression). Blind affect is not effective release. The anger must be connected to a simultaneous awareness of why, how, and at whom.

Procedure

The procedure is designed to be applied in the course of a psychodrama session in which the protagonist is blocked in his expression of anger toward an auxiliary ego. The protagonist is instructed to focus on the goal of getting his point communicated. He is informed that whenever he is interrupted he may silence the auxiliary ego by an agreed signal, such as extending his arm and saying, "Shut up!" The auxiliary ego's role is to interrupt the protagonist deliberately in midsentence with constant denials and disagreements but to stop talking the moment the protagonist applies the silencing signal. The silencing is to remain in effect until the director supercedes it with a given hand gesture, such as opening and closing the fingertips. Only then is the auxiliary ego to resume his interruptions. If the director uses the hand gesture frequently, the protagonist may need to apply his silencing signal many times before he can finish making his point.

When the scene has begun, the director uses his hand gesture to call for interruptions whenever the protagonist falls into inhibition; but when the protagonist's emotions flow freely, the silencing signal is allowed to remain in force. The procedure is terminated when it has reached a natural climax, and the group then discusses the experience.

EXAMPLE

A hypothetical example, somewhat condensed, might arise as follows: Rita, the protagonist, has been suffering headaches and a consequent disinclination to go to her job. She and her fiancé, Tommy, are both students and are living together. She works part-time in a bookstore, while Tommy is supposed to contribute to their household expenses by hand-tying fishing flies at home on a piecework basis. Instead he has been busying himself with piddling tasks, and Rita is exasperated. She plays down her feelings when she talks to him. In the first part of the drama Rita's confrontation scenes with Tommy have been tense and restrained, despite Rita's conscious attempt to purge herself of her bottled resentment. Other group members have suggested that her headaches are covertly hostile to Tommy as well as toward herself. They have pointed out that, by not working herself, she has been trying to manipulate Tommy into working out of sheer lack of money. She agrees with these interpretations on an intellectual level but says, "I have trouble expressing aggression." The director suggests that for the next scene Rita adopt as her goal making sure Tommy understands how much he procrastinates and how she feels about it. The general procedure of the silencing technique as described above has also been explained to the whole group. The letter "D" indicates the points at which the director signals the auxiliary ego to interrupt.

RITA: Hey, look Tommy. Now is a good time to work on the flies. Why don't you . . .

TOMMY: Later. What's a seven letter word for an Indonesian lily? Starts with a J.

RITA: Come on. Put that down. You've always got something else to do when it comes to tying flies. If it's not one thing, it's . . .

TOMMY: Are you kidding? I did a couple dozen more just the other day when you were out. I even . . .

RITA: (holding out her hand according to the signal): Shut up! That's not so. You haven't done any for at least two weeks even when you had off for Easter. Furthermore, you agreed. . . . (D)

TOMMY: I agreed to nothing. I only leave time to . . .

RITA (holding hand): Shut up, will you! You know perfectly well that you were supposed to make as much as I do. You told me you would have ten dozen finished before the weekend and instead you watered the plants three times in one day and watched Perry Mason for a whole hour and then you talked to Alan on the phone. It gets me so mad because . . .

TOMMY: I don't believe you. That kind of thing never bothers you. Someone must have told you that you're *supposed* to be upset. Some libber or . . .

RITA (holding hand): Shut up! Goddammit. You never listen to how I feel. This has had me so upset I can't tell you. If you go on like this what happens when we're married? What happens when we have a baby? It really scares me. You could end up sponging off of me as long as I put up with it. Do you think I want to go through what my mother went through? Either you straighten out and take some responsibility or you can damn well marry someone else!

Rita sits back and reflects, in angry tears.

RATIONALE FOR THE VARIOUS ELEMENTS OF THE PROCEDURE

The Auxiliary Ego's "Denials and Disagreements"

The auxiliary ego is instructed to directly contradict the protagonist. In this way the auxiliary can base what he says exactly on what the protagonist has said without diverting him from the content of his spontaneous ideas. Inhibited protagonists are often suggestible and eagerly follow any lead. They hesitate to take responsibility for initiating a new idea and prefer to talk about whatever the auxiliary ego might bring up. An impatient auxiliary ego working with an evasive and vague protagonist can easily resort to guesses and personal projections. The method of direct contradiction avoids this hazard, since the absolute value of the protagonist's ideas are left unchanged while the sign alone is reversed.

Also, the capacity of overcompliant protagonists to adhere to a given position is limited. They tend to back down easily, accepting any possible compromise through which they may save some shred of pride. Direct contradictions, however, offer no concession at all, leaving resistance or humiliation as the only alternatives. Any self-justification rather than contradiction on the part of the auxiliary ego opens the door for an evasion of the confrontation. Protagonist: "You always come home late." Auxiliary ego:

"Well you know how my boss is when we get all those back orders at once." This might be followed by, Protagonist: "Okay, but please try to call if you are held up . . ." in which the protagonist drops the issue of the lateness itself in deference to the auxiliary ego's defense. Protagonist: "You always come home so late." "No, I don't. I'm always home by 6:30." This polarizes the issue so the protagonist is forced to argue his case rather than agree to close the matter.

Evasive protagonists usually speak in generalities to avoid the factual details to which emotions may be attached. Without encouragement to move to specifics, many protagonists would continue an endless tirade of general accusations against the hated person. This hostility is dissociated from any clear content and provides little real catharsis or insight. "You never loved me! You always gave me a hard time! You were a mean son of a bitch!" sounds uninhibited enough, but it contains great resistance to any awareness of the acts or incidents in which the bothersome behavior was manifested. When the auxiliary ego denies the truth of these statements, he places the protagonist under the strongest impulsion to prove his case by citing chapter and verse. As: "You always borrow my stuff and never give it back." "Not so. I never like to borrow things from anyone." "Oh, no. What about the time that you . . . etc."

The resistance by generalization may be tenacious enough that contradicting the protagonist is not in itself sufficient to induce the emergence of specificity, and the auxiliary ego's technique may require further refinement. If, for example, the auxiliary ego merely states the inverse of the protagonist's general accusations, the conversation can easily bog down into a circular yes-you-do no-I-don't pattern. It is usually better for the auxiliary ego to state his denial as a positive assertion of the opposite rather than a mechanical negation of the protagonist's statement. To "you always ignore me," the auxiliary ego might get no-where with "I never ignore you." He might do better with something like, "My trouble is that I shower you with too much attention and now you are spoiled."

If the auxiliary ego tries to induce specificity by direct confrontation, he is also usually thwarted. A challenge such as, "So you say I always ignore you. Okay, tell me one time when I did" typically evokes further generalizations such as, "Well, you just always do," or even "I can't think of any examples. I guess I'm not too good at this. Can we stop now?" The auxiliary ego can phrase his own contradictions with a bit more specificity, being careful not to go so far as to lead the protagonist off his own track. If he were to reply, "How can you say I ignore you when I always bring roses home just for you?" he would undoubtedly divert the protagonist into totally inapplicable material. He may, however, move in the direction of specificity by references to situations known to be relevant to the protagonist's life or to specific situations of nearly universal applicability. For example, "Me ignore you? You know the first thing I do when I come home from work." Or, "Well you certainly can't say that I ignore you when we are at parties like some husbands do." Since most husbands come home from work and most couples attend parties from time to time, there is a good chance that these comments will strike off memories and move the protagonist toward specificity.

The Auxiliary Ego's Interruptions

The auxiliary ego is instructed to interrupt the protagonist continually. Already beset by internal inhibi-tions, the protagonist now finds himself faced with an op-ponent who constantly breaks in whenever he starts to say anything, not allowing him to culminate even those small acts of self-assertion which do manage to get past his inner blocks. For such protagonists, aggression can not be easily induced by suggestion nor generated by direct attack but can be effectively dammed up. Positive suggestion ("Go on and fight back!") results only in passive aggression. The hostility emerges in his failing at the exercise. The protagonist manages to end up feeling consciously that he can't do anything right and unconsciously hoping that the director feels likewise. Attempts to induce aggression by placing the protagonist under direct attack are also of little use. Counteraggression is swiftly repressed in accordance with a long-established defense pattern. Hostile stimuli generate little free aggression, and increasing the pressure only locks the inhibitory forces tighter. It is difficult indeed for such people ever to feel justified indignation, no matter how they are provoked.

Such individuals derive unusual satisfaction out of what would appear superficially to be a very meager reaction—a mumbled word of dissent or hint of irony in their tone of voice—but these inconspicuous safety valves are vital to the stability of the defensive system. When they are blocked by the auxiliary ego's interruptions, the internal pressure rises and seeks new outlets.

It is especially important that the auxiliary ego be instructed to interrupt the protagonist while he is in mid-sentence, for the protagonist's small safety-valve assertions can be culminated in an instant and allow the necessary release of tension. Once the protagonist has reduced the tension below his threshold of repressive capacity, it may be some time before he feels impelled to speak again. He tends to "forget" any further ideas he might have had and to fall into a listening mode. Interruption in mid-sentence blocks the vital act of communication by preventing the verbalization of the basic grammatical unit needed to transfer an idea. The usual relief of tension is denied, and inner pressure accumulates rapidly. The tendency to repress the content of the ideas is also minimized by the immediate timing. It is not easy to forget what you wanted to say when you are already half-way through saying it. The partly formed response Gestalt demands closure.

In this way an attitude of insistence is generated even in easily intimidated, overcompliant patients, and they become motivated to take recourse to the device which has been granted them to silence their adversary.

The Self-Releasing Nature of the Silencing Signal

The silencing signal is deliberately designed to be protagonist-actuated. Theoretically the silencing could be administered by the director, a double, or an auxiliary; but there are several advantages when the protagonist has the power by an act of will to release himself from verbal domination.

1. There is automatic self-regulation in which tension is released at the precise moment that the protagonist finds action more bearable than further repression. No critical timing or judgment is required of the director.

2. The protagonist cannot rely on an external lead but must accomplish the crucial act of volitional initiative.

3. If the control were left to an outside agent, the protagonist would risk feeling trapped, which would result in feeling panic or despair, rather than solution-oriented action.

4. Performing the silencing signal introduces the protagonist into an action mode which can then carry over into his behavior once he has gained the floor.

An occasional exception occurs when the protagonist seems so badly blocked that his tension rises beyond useful limits, but he cannot avail himself of the escape provided.

At such a time the director or double may administer the signal in his stead to release the stifled rage. Once he is assisted in this way, he can usually continue to use the device on his own.

The Silencing Signal

The established signal deliberately includes both a verbal (shut up!) and an action (extended hand) component. Its purpose is to engage both motor and cognitive functions in the act of release, helping to facilitate both modes in the free expression which follows.

The exact signal may be selected to convey aggression in itself, such as pointing the finger as if it were a gun and saying "bang." While sometimes effective, such a device may also engender excessive guilt and prove more inhibiting than liberating. The director can therefore weigh the appropriate degree of aggressivity inherent in the signal. He might select the verbal portion of the signal from along a scale such as "shut up, you bastard," "shut up," "quiet," "stop," "just a moment," "please." The physical gesture might vary similarly from a brandished fist to a raised forefinger. Sometimes one signal or another feels more natural to the protagonist. The signal phrase and gesture are selected to be as assertive as possible without making the protagonist feel too guilty to use it or unable to feel what he is saying. If a signal proves ineffective the director may need to change to a different one, but at any time the exact signal must be clear, specific, and understood by all parties. If the signal becomes ambiguous—for example, if the protagonist feels that either "wait" or "enough" will work—the protagonist may then also expect that yelling louder should work. At that point he begins to feel called upon to dominate the auxiliary ego with his personality, which he is certain he cannot do. He is caught up again in blockage and inadequacy. He gains confidence when he finds that a simple discreet gesture that cannot be done either well or poorly gives him absolute paralyzing power over his antagonist.

From time to time the director may wish to raise the intensity of the signal as the protagonist warms up. If the protagonist cannot bring himself to say "be quiet" directly to his father, he may begin with "kindly allow me to finish." But at the end of the scene he may be screaming, "Shut the hell up!" with conviction and emotion.

The Resumption of the Interruptions

While the protagonist has complete power to stop the auxiliary's interruptions, the effect is only temporary. As soon as the protagonist's spontaneity flags, the auxiliary ego is instructed to resume his interruptions. The protagonist is thus forced to use his weapon repeatedly. As the alternating interruptions and silencings proceed, a progressive escalation occurs in the intensity of emotion. It would seem that the act of emotional expression itself facilitates a fuller reaction to the next frustration. The first interruption blocks the protagonist's usual low-level expressions, forcing a slightly higher level of aggression. Once having transgressed the usual threshold of aggressiveness permitted, the protagonist discovers that the unconsciously feared disastrous results fail to materialize. He finds he has gotten away with it. If, at this moment, a fresh attempt is made to block his aggression before the old fears recongeal and negate the effect of the reality experience, the protagonist tends to maintain the newly opened channel of aggression and to open still another. It requires less courage to reuse his newly tested channel of aggression than was required to try it blindly for the first time. This frees the protagonist to apply his available courage to a still higher level of aggression.

After repeated exchanges, a sort of emotional explosion of anger tends to occur. Not only does the intensity of feeling grow, but many associated memories with detailed content emerge as well. Past incidents, deeply resented yet long suppressed and even fully repressed, come bubbling forth in the wave of rage.

The interrupting procedure is not, of course, continued indefinitely. A climax is reached when the protagonist's maximal psychodramatic aggression seems to result. If the auxiliary ego continues his interruptions beyond this point, the protagonist thankfully takes recourse to defenses that repudiate the therapeutic structure—such as breaking out of role or refusing to continue.

The decision as to when to resume the interruptions and when to allow the protagonist to ventilate may be maintained by the director and communicated to the auxiliary ego by hand signal. Sometimes, however, this decision may be safely delegated to a sensitive auxiliary ego whose role in the drama enables him to work more smoothly without the fractions of seconds of delay involved in the hand signals. Such an auxiliary ego, following basic guidelines, trusts his instincts as to how long each silencing will last. He may wish to have the period of silence very short to build up a high frustration level, but it must always be clear that the signal does work for a clearly perceptible interval so that the protagonist does not lose faith in its efficacy.

Choice of Auxiliary Ego

Besides all the usual considerations, the director must be sure to select an auxiliary ego who has the capacity to express free aggression at will, to dominate the protagonist verbally, and who clearly understands the purpose of the procedure.

Resistance

Needless to say, the forces of resistance are usually too ingenious to be foiled by the rote application of this technique. It therefore becomes the role of the director, after having set the technical machinery in progress, to observe whether and in what way the protagonist manages to defeat the agreed purpose of the procedure. He may then judiciously intervene to describe the form of resistance to the protagonist, who may then be able to overcome it spontaneously. At other times, the director may supplement his description with interpretation or further directorial advice. Whenever the director finds himself opposing rather than merely interpreting any resistance, it is essential that his role remain clearly that of a partner to the health-seeking side of the patient, available for suggestions and techniques that might be of help against a common unconscious adversary. He must never become an opponent of the conscious self trying to convince the patient of something for his own good.

Interventions are best phrased to minimize the authoritarian position of the director: "I think it might help if you spoke louder" is better than "talk louder" for protagonists who are either resentful of being told what to do or who fall into easy compliance and leader dependency.

In order to minimize manipulation, it helps to expose the therapeutic goal as much as possible. Even such a simple direction as "louder" might lead some protagonists to wonder, "What is he trying to do? What will he trick me into?" In such a case it might be necessary to phrase the direction, "I think if you spoke very loudly it might help overcome that wishy-washy quality you were complaining about."

Interventions should not be too frequent; each scene should have a chance to run its course. Too many interventions, regardless of how astute, detract from the dramatic flow. The protagonist also comes to feel that he must be doing poorly, since the director must constantly correct him.

Directorial comments should also be delivered in as few words as possible. Nothing breaks the buildup of emotion more than for the director to become wordy and over-intellectual himself.

Typical Resistances

CONFUSION AND REPRESSING THE OBJECTIVE. It frequently occurs that the protagonist goes mentally blank. His motivation fades, and he may even forget completely what he had been trying to accomplish in the scene. In lesser degree, he may mouth clichés or perseverate a single idea. He may stand dumb, waiting to react to the auxiliary ego's initiative. The resulting scene is dull and directionless as if the protagonist were continuing only because he felt he should. He may try to disguise his confusion by merely reacting rather than acting. Since the auxiliary ego does not introduce new content, the protagonist must basically take the lead in the conversation or it soon grinds to a halt. The auxiliary ego speaks to interrupt—but only to interrupt. If the protagonist is silent, he falls silent also. The problem is aggravated after any detailed directorial intervention, or when any complexity arises in the dramatic interaction. A direct interpretation of the defense, such as "perhaps you don't *want* to remember," would only introduce more threat and confusion.

It may be of help, however, to restate the protagonist's forgotten objective. Thus, when the protagonist drops the initiative, forgets what he is trying to do, or becomes generally confused, the director can simply remind him of his goal. The goal is generally best stated in terms of producing a particular influence on the auxiliary player. The director might say to the confused protagonist, "Remember that you set your task in this scene to get your dad to admit that he never paid your allowance on time. If you haven't gotten him to admit it yet, you might keep trying." More often, the director need not mention the goal himself but simply ask the protagonist to reiterate the objective of his behavior. With some protagonists it has been helpful to ask several times in the course of a scene, "What, again, were you trying to accomplish here?" Then the protagonist was able to resume.

While it is useful to help clarify the protagonist's goal, it is inevitably counterproductive to suggest any means for accomplishing the goal. With the "what" of the protagonist's goal clear, his opportunity is best left open for creative variation in the "how" of the pursuit.

SHORT SENTENCES.   Occasionally the protagonist will discover that by speaking in a very short single sentence he can finish his thought before the auxiliary has a chance to interrupt. He can thus gain a premature release before the emotion has had a chance to dam up. The auxiliary ego may be able to outmaneuver this tack of the resistance by watching closely and breaking in at the first movement of the protagonist's lips in preparation for speech. More directly, a simple description of the process may enable the protagonist to abandon this method of defeating the technique. "I think it would work better if you use your 'shut up' signal instead of squeezing in what you have to say so fast." Or, "I noticed that you are pulling those one-liners again so that our interrupting trick doesn't work."

FAILURE TO USE THE SILENCING SIGNAL.   Some protagonists rather than use the silencing signal allow themselves to be constantly interrupted and wait for the auxiliary ego to finish his speech. They then patiently try to speak again but are again interrupted. These patients tend to see themselves as unwilling victims of domination. When it is

pointed out that they are cooperating in their own domination by not using a power available to them, they are faced
with a contradiction in their self-perception. As the self-
defeating pattern is ego alien, they usually begin availing
themselves of the silencing signal on the next try. In any
case, the masochistic motive can be exposed and explored.

OVERLAPPING.   Other protagonists refuse to be interrupted by indulging in a screaming contest where both
parties talk at once and no one listens. These patients are
indeed stimulated into strong hostile verbalization by the
procedure, but by not using the silencing signal they never
allow themselves the feeling of being heard. They experience only ventilation, not communication. The director's
intervention might be, "You seem to be having less trouble
telling her what you think than you used to. Remember you
also have the power to make her listen if you want to see
what that feels like."

INAPPROPRIATE LAUGHTER.   If the director mentions this
defense prematurely, he may be seen by the protagonist
and the group as compulsively serious and prohibitive toward reasonable levity. Persistent defensive laughter
should, however, be described and interpreted.

A general interpretation is usually less threatening for
the protagonist than if he were singled out. The director
might say something like, "Trying to be more assertive is
something new for Al, so naturally it is difficult for him to
keep from smiling just at the moment of anger. If everybody laughs with him at that point, it is tempting for him
to give up on being aggressive at all." When the group does
not join in the laughter, the interpretation might be tact-
fully directed toward the protagonist alone. For example,
"(Laughing) That really is quite funny, I must admit. At the
same time, I noticed that the side of you that wants to avoid
the experience of anger always finds a humorous twist

when you are just about to get mad. Let's see what happens when we try this scene again."

LONG PAUSES.   Another resistance is simply delay. Sometimes one can hear emotion begin to rise in the protagonist's voice; then he suddenly stops and waits for the feeling to subside. Only after he has pulled himself together will he speak again, pause again, and so on. The protagonist may be totally unaware of this. When it is carefully pointed out, he may overcome the tendency spontaneously. At other times, he may find the following device productive. The director suggests that he makes a point of talking continuously. He may give quotations, repetitions, lies, even nonsense syllables, so long as his vocal cords never cease vibrating. Freed from the requirement to make sense, most protagonists can produce such a continuous stream. When a double joins with them temporarily in the noisemaking, it seems to prime the pump of the reticent. Curiously enough, when this method is used in the context of the present procedure the protagonist's stream of speech quickly loses its nonsensical character. The protagonist soon finds himself again saying the same kinds of things he had been saying before but without the inhibiting pauses, so that the emotion mounts quickly.

BODY INHIBITIONS.   The protagonist may show marked restraint in his posture or physical movements and gestures. He may also post himself on the stage at a point very distant from his partner to lessen the intensity of the contact. While such body defenses constitute a separate subject, there is one technique that has been useful when such inhibitions are exhibited in the course of the method being described. An auxiliary ego is introduced to restrict the freedom of movement of the protagonist. He may hold the protagonist's arms tightly from behind, allowing the patient to move his arms only enough to accomplish the necessary silencing gesture. This procedure follows the principle of treating inhibition with further restriction to accumulate frustration. In this way, the source of inhibition is externalized in the drama to give the protagonist a tangible force against which to struggle. This temporarily converts the inhibitory force into a dramatically real force, allowing active interaction with it. As the protagonist struggles against the confining of his arms, his anger rises. It is as if the protagonist delegates the role of his intrapsychic binder to an auxiliary ego in order to free himself to accept the exclusive role of that part of himself which struggles for freedom.

Sometimes the externalization of the inhibitory force can be accomplished by psychodramatic convention alone, without the introduction of physical contact or of an auxiliary ego. An imaginary iron gate or glass wall might be set up between the players, which the protagonist may pound on. Since the protagonist realizes that this barrier prevents him from assaulting the other person, he can throw himself more fully into an unrestrained attack with less fear of his own violence.

THE VOICE. It is obvious that loudness of voice is related to self-assertion and aggression, and the suggestion to speak up or even to yell sometimes facilitates genuine angry affect. Unfortunately, some protagonists unconsciously block this capacity and literally cannot yell at will. Others holler on command but do so mechanically, so that the associated emotions do not accompany the increased amplitude of the voice. It is therefore usually more effective to make directorial changes in the situation. The auxiliary ego might be made hard of hearing, or the auxiliary ego and the protagonist might be placed at opposite ends of a large room. When the protagonist then uses loudness as a method of arriving at his goal of communication, it is more likely to carry genuine feeling than when loudness is made a goal in itself.

The Use of Modeling

The various role-modeling techniques are effective in overcoming resistance in the present procedure. The director may call on members of the group to demonstrate alternative, usually more aggressive, forms of behavior, which the protagonist might then observe and try to repeat. Some directors may use their own emotions for subliminal or conscious role-modeling. A flashing eye, a brandished fist, or a slightly raised voice, while giving directions or in referring to the person in the antagonist role, sometimes sets a tone that the protagonist may incorporate in his own behavior. Other directors may offer a formal demonstration of alternative behavior for the protagonist.

Some patients feel that only after they have seen another person express aggressiveness in the drama can they accept the director's statement that aggressiveness in the drama is really letigimate and appropriate. Unless someone else goes first, they assume that while self-assertion is given lip service, an underlying restrictive value system is really operating. Such a patient would rather be considered a poor actor than be considered a fool or outrageous for expressing real anger. Asked why he was so reticent, one such patient said, "I'm trying to figure out the unwritten rules."

Some people are unaggressive because of having been cowed into submission during their formative years. Others were raised in generally inhibited families. The latter type grow up feeling that the expression of aggressive impulse is not something that will be punished but something that people just don't do. They may have a very limited repertoire of aggressive behavior, language, and gesture, and role modeling is needed to provide them with new possible ways of expressing anger.

Some cautions in the use of role modeling include:

1. Undervaluing the role of unconscious motivation in favor of conscious teaching.

2. Providing too easy a solution for the protagonist on which he can come to depend rather than exercise his own creativity.

3. Humiliating rather than inspiring the protagonist.

After someone else demonstrates how much more aggressive he can be, the protagonist may feel unable to live up to the previous demonstration and be less inclined than ever to try.

chapter 4

IMPLOSIVE THERAPY

Thomas G. Stampfl, Ph.D.

Whenever I address a large audience and a microphone is hung around my neck, the experience reminds me of a patient I once treated who had strong suicidal tendencies to hang herself as her sister had done before her. In order to facilitate the realism of the scenes involving hanging that I planned to have my patient experience in imagery, I hung a microphone around her neck as someone might hang one around mine. This may be viewed as a redintegrative process.

Redintegration is extensively used in implosive therapy (IT). One stimulus or cue activates related stimuli or cues. When combined with the principles of stimulus generalization, response-mediated generalization, experimental extinction, and generalization of extinction organized in terms of a two-process theory of learning (Mowrer 1947; 1956; 1960*a,b*), the basis is laid for an effective method of treatment. The fact that having a microphone hung around my neck redintegrated thoughts and images of this patient represents the redintegrative process that I was trying to obtain in her—they are the same order of phenomena.

As I shall explain in greater detail below, implosive therapy involves the reproduction of stimulus configurations that are derived from conditioning events of the past. The emotional reactions conditioned to these stimuli presumably control the problem behaviors observed in the patient. Theoretically, the repetition of these stimulus configurations in the absence of unconditioned reinforcement should lead to the extinction of the emotional reactions conditioned to them. So it is important to reproduce the stimulus configurations as accurately and completely as possible.

Implosive therapy, then, is a behavioral therapy that utilizes the principle of extinction in the treatment of deviant behavior. In this view the symptoms and/or problems of the patient are seen as motivated by conditioned anxiety and/or conditioned anger reactions that were acquired as a result of past experiences involving punishment, frustration, and pain.

Main Steps of Treatment by Implosive Therapy

Before going into detail concerning the theoretical basis of the therapy, let me summarize the main steps of the procedures use in IT and then illustrate these procedures with actual clinical cases.

First, the therapist usually conducts two diagnostic interviews with the patient. At this time, the therapist seeks to answer the following questions: What is the patient avoiding? What might he be avoiding? What makes him anxious or angry? What might make him anxious or angry? What are the characteristics of the patient's aversive conditioning history in relation to the socialization process, peer group and sibling experiences, and natural events of a traumatic nature? Ten basic classes of stimuli representing four categories of cues (Stampfl and Levis 1967) include almost all of the stimuli or cues listed by the therapist during the interviews.

The steps listed below summarize the entire treatment procedure:

1. Diagnostic interviews: specification of aversive stimuli.

2. Imagery: the patient is trained in the use of imagery.

3. Implosive extinction sessions: the therapist directs imaginal scenes in which the aversive stimuli are included.

4. Hypothesized approximations: the therapist makes clinical guesses concerning stimuli that cannot be precisely identified.

5. Homework assignments: the patient is asked to practice in imagery the aversive scenes used during the implosive extinction sessions.

6. Repetition: the procedure is repeated until the main problems of the patient are markedly reduced or eliminated. Typically, marked improvement occurs in 1 to 15 one-hour sessions.

I have a tape that illustrates how the principles may be applied specifically to the treatment of the human patient. The young woman is troubled by a long-standing phobia of bugs and a fear of marriage. She is able to date easily, but when a particular relationship progresses to the point where serious consideration of marriage occurs, it becomes very aversive for her. At such times she feels entangled, trapped. She becomes irritable and quickly breaks the relationship completely. On the other hand, she can enjoy dating the same man repeatedly over a long period of time so long as he doesn't talk seriously about the possibility of marriage. Also, she has difficulty asserting herself and correspondingly finds others taking advantage of her in her daily life. The basis for this appears to depend on her fear of aggressive behavior by herself or others. She becomes anxious even with commonplace gossiping.

In therapy, then, I am going to try to reproduce what she is afraid of. She is afraid of bugs. What kind of bug is it that frightens her most, what is it specifically about the bug that she finds so alarming? If she particularly dislikes crawling bugs, she is going to be exposed to crawling bugs. If she is afraid of bugs that have a negative attitude toward her, that hate her and hold her responsible for having committed terrible crimes, animated bugs expressing precisely this point of view are what she is going to get. I will keep this sequence going and in the meantime try to bring in some other things that she is afraid of also.

Remember that two diagnostic interviews preceded this first IT session. A good deal has been discovered concerning the details of her three main problems and the relationship between these and her conditioning history. Also, the patient has already been trained in imagery.

Synopsis of IT tape: Actual implosion begins with the therapist's instruction to imagine herself reliving a disturbing repetitious dream "as though it's actualized into reality." The patient enters a room and sees a jewel glittering enticingly on a white curtain. She approaches the jewel, but when she reaches out to grab it she realizes that it is actually a repellent black bug. The therapist dwells on the details of the insect's appearance and the intensity of the patient's revulsion.

This recurrent dream was reported by the patient in the diagnostic interviews. The dream is used as a jump-off point to introduce other sets of aversive stimuli.

The patient reports the impulse to either smash the bug or to flee the room; the second option is her preference. This imagined behavior is vetoed by the therapist. She is instructed to see herself striking the insect with her shoe. But an odd thing happens; the bug is not destroyed but instead actually increases in size. The patient realizes that the entire room is filled with bugs. She goes around hitting them with her shoe and they all become bigger. She sees now that there are too many bugs for her to escape from the room. She tiptoes around gingerly, trying to avoid them.

A bug begins to crawl up her leg. Provoked into desperation by the accelerating fearfulness of the sequence, she struggles to leave the room but is overwhelmed and falls to the floor, where the insects cover her. They crawl all over her skin and begin to penetrate within her through her ears. So thoroughly is she immersed in them that she "can't even see herself." Now she notices the bugs' eyes; they are all regarding her with a vicious, evil look. The bugs hate her; they have a mission to destroy her. Why do they feel this way? "The bugs say that you are guilty of all sorts of terrible things." The penetration of the bugs into the patient's body is intensified. They march into her mouth, ears, and nose en masse, forming a swarming horde within her. The patient is instructed that this condition is permanent. She will always be filled with the hostile insects. She imagines herself living in the world outside the room accompanied by them—driving a car, going to the theater, always with the hateful bugs tearing at her insides.

Again, the diagnostic interviews had revealed that somehow an association between bugs and feeling guilty about "bad" behavior was present. Some of the conditioning events that made this association plausible were remembered by the patient for the first time following several implosive sessions.

The patient is returned to the room of her dream. There she is presented with a giant bug, a king bug dominant over all the others and "even a little larger than you." The huge insect slowly approaches her, the hideous details of his appearance becoming more and more evident as he comes closer and closer. His eyes are full of hatred and accusation. Within three feet of her, he extends a tentacle and draws her into an inexorable embrace. She feels the numerous tiny hairs of his body quivering against her skin as he kisses her repeatedly. Finally, the patient herself begins to change into a bug. She tries to fight the transformation, but there is nothing she can do. "It's an irreversible process." She feels hairs sprouting from her skin and the distortion of her limbs and torso.

In the remainder of the first session, the patient is married to the bug in a formal ceremony complete with a bug minister and all-bug wedding party. With cinemascopic veracity and attention to detail, she imagines herself living with the insect who, sure enough, turns out to be a particularly cruel and vicious bug husband. Later on, human figures will be used as her anxieties are approached on a generalization gradient. As is often the case, this patient's conditioning history seems to explain her idiosyncratic associations; events from her past appear to link fear of bugs, guilt, and fear of marriage very neatly.

The principles followed in this relatively simple case may be applied to the treatment of almost any behavioral disorder: compulsives, obsessives, individuals with conflicts centering around dependence, or even the delusional behavior of the psychotic.

In all cases one asks what is the patient avoiding. What are the stimuli, the product of the patient's conditioning history, that will now generate the affect which controls the symptomatic behavior? When the answer has been hypothesized, the stimuli are presented repeatedly to the patient mainly through the use of imagery. The result is the extinction of his learned emotionality.

FURTHER CASE ILLUSTRATIONS

Take for example the question of an individual whose behavior has become sufficiently grotesque as to cause alarm among his friends. Essentially, this man is suspicious that his wife is having an affair with somebody else. This person is so disturbed by his suspicions that he quits his job in order to watch his wife. He forces her to account for every move she makes outside of his presence and insists with equal vehemence that she swear repeatedly that she not only is not now having an affair with another man, but never has and never will. He even goes so far as to arrange a lie detector test. The significance of the man's morbid suspiciousness is suggested by the nature of the cleaning rituals in which he indulges subsequent to intercourse. A focal point of these is the examination of the skin of the penis; he tends to see red spots there. In the light of this, it may be understood that he fears venereal disease and thinks that he may catch it from his wife after she has contracted it from someone else.

In an implosive sequence, this individual is instructed to imagine his penis clearly inflamed subsequent to intercourse with his wife. Then it changes colors, becoming yellowish green; the skin sags and peels; ultimately it will fall off altogether. He rushes to question his wife, who then reveals that she has had extensive and prolonged extramarital relations with a veritable battery of diseased men. In fact, she produces a stack of medical records from famous medical clinics describing in detail the severity of her lovers' various afflictions.

Of course, the description of this case is drastically

oversimplified, but it illustrates the basic principle of avoidance in mildly delusional behavior.

Consider a patient who has elaborate handwashing rituals, turns light switches on and off with his elbows, and displays a niggardly character out of all proportion to the actual financial means that he enjoyed. A specific stimulus configuration that elicits his symptomatic behavior is that of a wastebasket. The mere sight of the basket is sufficient to trigger his handwashing compulsion, presumably because it reminds him of dirt. The implosion of the patient, then, begins with the presentation of a wastebasket in imagery.

The patient sees the basket and experiences the urge to leave the room to engage in his purification ritual. Instead of this, he is told to imagine himself approaching the basket and sticking his hand into it. Now it is clear that the basket he fears is not clean but very dirty. Since the therapist does not know what specific sort of effluvium the patient finds especially offensive, the patient's hand, when withdrawn from the receptacle, is covered by all the likelier candidates: mucus, saliva, defecation, vomit. These substances are described in minute detail; the greenish glitter of the mucus, the ooziness of the defecation as they drip in slow motion from the patient's fingers. His emotionality at this point is very high, but the implosive sequence has hardly begun. Next he is told to visualize himself licking off his fingers as a child gulps down an ice cream cone. The stuff slides down his throat and coagulates into a poisonous lump.

Subsequently the patient is transferred to scenes evocative of toilet-training experiences. An outhouse, with its odors, flies, and stains, is chosen as the setting to accentuate dirt stimuli. Ultimately the patient slips through the seat, landing with a splat in the mass of fecal material below. Finally, he makes his home in a septic tank: he eats, sleeps, studies, and even throws cocktail parties there. This sort of exposure is continued until a substantial decrease in the patient's anxiety is achieved. He becomes adjusted to his life underneath the outhouse, selecting with a connoisseur's eye the gooiest, slimiest pieces of fecal material for his meals. Eventually he can think about dirt without negative effect.

The patient's symptomatic behavior is understood as the avoidance of emotionally charged imagery. The sight of the basket redintegrates potentially the thought of dirt and contamination, an association that is aborted by the hand-washing compulsion. The implosive therapist defeats this avoidance response by imposing directly on the patient the imagery he is hypothesized to be avoiding, an inference that may be made from the nature of his symptom.

Of course, the actual therapy is more involved than this brief description would suggest. First, there were a number of serious debilities other than his compulsions. Secondly, many other themes were interrelated with his compulsions (for example, sex and guilt), and there were a number of inferences culled from the conditioning history obtained during his diagnostic interviews. So my description represents only a small fraction of his total therapy.

The avoidance principle is a central one. Thus, if a patient suffers from a bathtub phobia and always wears a life preserver when she takes a bath, it should be clear that having her take a bath (in imagery) without wearing the life preserver will represent a stimulus configuration that she is avoiding. If part of her avoidance appears to be based on a feeling she experiences that the bathtub may be bottomless, then a more complete stimulus configuration would include the bottomless nature of the bathtub. Furthermore, what actual conditioning events might have conferred "bottomless" characteristics to bathtubs? It should be clear also that these events would be replayed in imagery as precisely as possible. Indeed, the experienced clinician will trace an associative linkage of a variety of themes related to her phobia. Whatever is aversive in this associative linkage is reproduced in the therapy.

The utilization of the avoidance principle is fully applicable to hospitalized psychotic patients. Take, for example, a paranoid schizophrenic patient who has been hospitalized continuously for five years and has had a long succession of hospital admissions for twenty-five years. The main delusion is that his persecutors have plotted to have the Internal Revenue Service send him to the electric chair. To complicate matters, he also has a sexual deviation involving getting his head defecated on that has lasted for over forty years. The therapy is somewhat more complex for such a patient; nevertheless, it is fully possible to treat both sets of symptoms in terms of the avoidance principle.

Many successfully treated cases include a larger number of hospitalized schizophrenics and psychotically depressed patients. They include one severely regressed schizophrenic and one post-surgical psychosis. A fairly large number of sexual deviations and other personality disorders have also been treated by IT methods. Clinically, excellent results appear to occur in most cases. I shall refer to some of the systematic research later.

THEORY

As early as 1939, O. Hobart Mowrer suggested that the Freudian interpretation of symptom formation as a response to the anxiety produced by intrapsychic danger signals was similar to the conditioning of fear in infrahuman animals as illustrated in the typical laboratory avoidance experiment.

Following Mowrer's lead, Shoben (1949), Dollard and Miller (1950), and many other theorists made extensive use of conditioning principles in discussing the problems of human psychopathology. The theoretical discussion centered mainly on the classical conditioning of emotional reactions such as fear or anxiety as a means of explaining neurotic behavior. The acquired anxiety then functions as a motivator of behavior. The instrumental symptomatic behavior and defenses of the neurotic are interpreted as avoidance responses reinforced by anxiety reduction. Anxiety reduction occurs when the organism terminates or minimizes the stimuli generating the anxiety reaction.

Though a detailed theoretical analysis was made of the phenomena related to the problem, little or no effort was invested in an attempt to modify existing therapeutic strategies in accordance with the theoretical analysis. However, experimental psychologists were extremely active in conducting laboratory research in avoidance learning with infrahuman subjects. Over a period of years, a great many avoidance experiments were published in scientific journals. It would take me too far afield to attempt to discuss the significant laboratory research on avoidance learning done by workers such as Hobart Mowrer, Neal Miller, Judson Brown, Richard Solomon, Leon Kamin, Abraham Black, Robert Brush, Ray Denny, Russel Church, Harold Kalish, James Carlson, the McAllisters, and a very large number of others. This laboratory research was extremely important, for it provided the guidelines and confidence for human application.

DEVELOPMENT OF IMPLOSIVE THERAPY

Implosive therapy was originally developed in response to a single question. The question consisted simply of asking what a therapy would be like if it reflected as faithfully as possible the operations of the experimental psychologist when he subjected lower animals to extinction procedures in the animal laboratory.

Laboratory studies revealed that one way to eliminate avoidance responding was simply to apply the operation of Pavlovian (experimental) extinction. This finding was confirmed repeatedly in dozens of experimental studies. When combined with the two-factor model of avoidance learning, a set of procedures for modifying the maladaptive behavior of human patients is relatively easy to obtain; one reproduces stimuli similar to the stimuli that are mediating the affect that drives the patients' symptomatic behavior. In the absence of the unconditioned stimulus, the emotionality conditioned to the mediating stimulus will extinguish if elicited persistently. Consequently, the maladaptive behavior manifests a corresponding reduction.

If one emulates the behavior of the experimenter in the laboratory four characteristics are immediately apparent; he is active, persistent, direct, and does not require subjective validation.

The Experimenter Is Active

In imposing extinction trials on lower animals, the experimenter forces their exposure to precisely that which, in terms of their own behavior, they would be most likely to avoid. A buzzer, for example, that has been paired with electric shock becomes frightening and aversive to the rat. The experimenter simply arranges the rat's environment so that it cannot escape the perception of this aversive stimulus. Similarly, the implosive therapist makes use of systematic techniques to encourage his patient to confront precisely that which he least desires to recognize, that which disturbs and frightens him, by actively reproducing such stimuli.

The Experimenter Is Persistent

The experimenter exposes the animal to aversive stimuli as many times as necessary until extinction occurs. Repetition is the essence of his operation. Initially the rat will react to the presentation of the aversive stimulus with a high degree of emotionality. However, with repetition a marked decrease in emotionality occurs. The effect is similar to the phenomenon of the dissipation of emotional impact that attends the repeated viewings of even the most effective horror movies. Even the gruesome films made by auto insurance companies to frighten errant drivers into safer driving habits can be counted on to bore the projectionist. The point is, repeated exposure to anything that frightens or angers one without the unconditioned stimulus will lead to extinction. The implosive therapist persists in reproducing aversive stimuli until this effect is achieved.

The Experimenter Is Direct

The experimenter reproduces for the lower organism the perceptual characteristics of the conditioned aversive stimulus. No attempt is made to deal with the rat on a higher level of abstraction; the animal is not requested to explain how he feels about the traumatic experiences of his past. Instead the experimenter simply forces exposure to the relevant stimulus, the buzzer, through the arrangement of the extinction trial. Transposing this operation to the treatment of humans, imagery was chosen as the medium most faithful to the patient's conditioning history from which the emotionality that drives his maladaptive behavior derives. Aversive conditioning events of the past, ranging from the various punishments of the socialization process, conflicts with peers or parents, to natural events that resulted in injury are seen to leave in the nervous system the potential for the redintegration of the affect that was experienced at the time of the event. The symptomatic behavior is understood primarily as the avoidance of this redintegration. This is consistent with Mowrer's revised two-factor theory of learning (Mowrer 1960 *a,b*), with its emphasis on the image as the mediator of behavior; it is argued that the agitation of the patient's pictorial memory through imagery is the most direct route to the emotionality that is to be evoked and extinguished.

Subjective Validation

Finally, the experimenter does not require any subjective validation of his treatment's effectiveness from his laboratory animal other than observable emotional reactions and behavior change. The implosive therapist makes no attempt to convince his patient of a particular implosive sequence's truth. If, for example, a patient is instructed to imagine himself being attracted sexually to his mother, the question of his real life attachment to her or his lack of one is not for that reason occasioned. Even if the patient himself suggests a connection between the implosive sequence and his personal history, a problematical discussion is usually avoided; I neither agree nor disagree. Like the experimenter, the implosive therapist is concerned with the simple presentation of aversively conditioned stimuli in the absence of the unconditioned stimulus as a means of behavior modification.

Watching the therapy being demonstrated, it sometimes seems as though the therapist is sadistically attempting to inflict psychic pain on his patient, as if the latter's humanity were no concern of the former. In fact, there are two levels of communication in IT. On one the patient is treated with all the dignity that should be accorded a human being. On the other, it is the strategy of the therapy to employ whatever procedures are effective in actually helping the patient. In fact, to do less seems unethical. The therapist's role is somewhat like that of a dentist or surgeon who is highly motivated to do the very best for his patients.

The procedures used in the therapy do seem to be highly effective. I have had extensive clinical experience, dating from 1957, in using the therapy. My early co-workers, George Golias, Robert Hogan, and Donald Levis, have had only a year or two less experience. A fairly large number of therapists, such as Richard Carrera, Gerald Rosenbaum, Patrick Boudewyns, Mike Tomaro, and James Gumina, have in the past and are now using implosive techniques. Many additional students have been trained in the method over the past several years. Certainly, based on clinical impression, the consensus of those employing the therapy is that it produces good clinical results.

If one adopts a scientific view of therapy, though, it seems that clinical impression is not an adequate basis for evaluation. However convincing a therapeutic method may appear to the individual clinician, the scientific problem of objective validation remains.

In this respect there exists now four published experimental studies of IT with clinical patients. All of these studies utilized control groups, objective criteria of change, and statistical evaluation of results. One study (Hogan 1966) treated hospitalized psychotic inpatients. Levis and Carrera (1967) treated clinical outpatients, and Boulougouris, Marks, and Marset (1971) treated phobic inpatients and outpatients. The most recent evaluation is that of Boudewyns and Wilson (1972) who used VA hospital patients as subjects. In each of these studies, statistically significant differences in outcome were found between IT and control groups. The experimental evidence of a scientific nature existing at the present time in which clinical patients are used as subjects definitely appears to support IT as an effective method of treatment. Hopefully, much additional research will be done in the future.

Additional Case Material

Synopsis of demonstration case: The subject is a woman. In her opening remarks she explains that her problem is the inability to swim. Although she has taken lessons several times, she is unable to learn the skill because of the great emotionality that overwhelms her when she is immersed in water beyond her knees. At such times she panics, screams, and clutches at anyone nearby. The subject expresses a strong desire to learn to swim. In fact so great is her frustration at not being able to that she refuses to live near the ocean because it reminds her of the situation.

The principal conditioning event from which the anxiety that prevents her from swimming derives is readily accessible to her memory: when she was eight years old, she was nearly drowned at the seashore by a friend who suddenly thrust her head under water and held it there. The subject explains that her family had gone to the beach for a picnic on that occasion; her four elder siblings were swimming out further from the shore when her friend, a large girl much bigger than the subject, assaulted her. The subject thought at the time that she was dying—in fact, that she was already dead—but she was rescued by her mother. A month later, the fat girl who had held her down died of a burst appendix.

The subject expresses the belief that the emotional concomitants of this experience had already been worked through; the only residue is her inability to swim. The therapist questions her as to the precise relationship between her anxiety and the stimulus configurations of the water. Her panic, it is found, is associated most specifically with the feeling of being immersed in a lot of water, its tactual heaviness. In search of the family context within which her trauma might be understood, the therapist asks about her relationships to her siblings and learns that she was the "pet." This status is associated with her memory of being awarded a particularly choice piece of meat at the dinner table in preference to all the other children.

The subject is requested to close her eyes and asked, "What do you see?" She spontaneously recalls the scene just mentioned in which she is awarded the prime piece of chicken. She is asked to imagine the sequence vividly, with attention to detail in the various senses; the smell of the chicken, the hardness of the wooden chair, the sight of her siblings looking at her enviously, as well as her own emotions at the time. Various neutral scenes are now introduced; the subject is asked to imagine herself back in high school and then in elementary school. She is asked to pay attention to the physical sensations in her stomach and shoulders as she does so. Finally, she pictures herself as a champion tennis player. She is unable to see herself as a champion swimmer.

Now the subject is exposed to imagery that becomes progressively more implosive. She is returned to the scene where she receives the best piece of meat. She feels modest, humble, but elated inside. Her siblings look at her; they are sullen, resentful. After the meal, the children play various games. Her mother casually mentions that they will go to a picnic at the seashore this afternoon. Preparations for the affair are made; the family packs into the station wagon and rolls off to the beach. The subject imagines the car's occupants and the changing nature of the landscape. Her emotions are quite cheerful, as the situation warrants, but there is a certain component of uneasiness there too. It is an undercurrent of anxiety, an apprehension that things are not the way they should be.

The patient recalls at this point that there was a circumstance at the time that would explain such a negative sentiment. A friend of hers from school had undergone a physical transformation through plastic surgery, the essence of which was that her nose was shortened. In the light of her friend's radically improved appearance, the subject had resolved to "have something cut off too;" she had had her hair shorn. This in turn had proved to be a negative experience. Besides this, a typical anxiety to be found in a young child who has not yet learned to swim might be that he will be unable to do so because of innate stupidity. The subject is instructed to feel this: that she is just too dumb to learn to swim. Her siblings will play in the water while she, dejected, will remain on the beach. "Won't that be sweet revenge for the meat you got at the dinner table?" Because of her inherent incapacity, to persist in the attempt at swimming will certainly be the cause of her death. Despite this presentiment, the patient vows to herself to do precisely that, to persist at the task though it means her death. The therapist dwells on this fatalistic determination.

The subject arrives at the beach. Everyone swims out to the raft except her. She resolves to swim there too, even though she knows it will kill her. She steps into the water; it gradually rises past her ankles, her knees, up to her waist. She continues to progress deeper and deeper until suddenly an unseen hand grabs her and holds her under water. She is immersed, drowning; she coughs water and wildly questions the impulse that led her to tempt fate in this fashion. She dies; she rolls in the water like a bloated fish. She can hear the sirens and see the flashing lights as she is dragged back to the beach. There she is surrounded by her family, her mother weeping; her siblings also weep, but underneath they may be smirking with satisfaction.

The synopsis represents approximately forty minutes of treatment time in which diagnostic interviewing, training in neutral imagery, and implosive extinction trials were included.

chapter 5

INTENSE FEELING THERAPY

Sidney Rose, M.D.

For years all psychoanalytic schools have maintained that emotion must emerge in the therapeutic process if insights are to be effective. They are correct in theory; but in practice they have failed because what they have identified as feeling is simply not sufficiently intense.

Not until the appearance of Janov's book *The Primal Scream* (1970) did the theme of opening up the whole being to the fullest expression of the deepest and most primitive feelings come to the fore. While strong affect had been allowed to emerge by therapists using catharisis and abreaction, apparently none used emotional flooding as a deliberate therapeutic tactic.

Primarily through his early interest in hypnosis, Freud was well acquainted with abreaction and catharsis, but what he referred to is merely a pale version of what occurs when intense emotion is allowed to take over and the whole per-

---

Portions of this chapter appeared in different form in *Groups,* the Newsjournal of the Eastern Group Psychotherapy Society.

son participates with crying, screaming, and powerful bodily movements. If Freud, in his later work, had encouraged his patients beyond verbal free associations, if he had encouraged them to talk in the present tense in order to elicit more nonverbal expressions of feelings and bodily participation, he would have discovered what Janov did— that is, that this emotional flooding of the patient permitted the earliest memories to surface.

Intense feeling therapy follows the format of Janov. (The term "primal therapy" is not used in deference to Janov, who feels that therapists should not use this form of treatment unless they have been treated and trained by him.) What is crucial about this new approach is the regressed state into which the patient learns to enter voluntarily. It is referred to as "primaling."

The therapy consists of two parts. The first is a three-week crash program during which the patient is seen daily in open-ended sessions lasting as much as three hours. In this three-week intensive period, the patient is isolated in a hotel, forbidden to see anyone, and not allowed to smoke, watch television, or indulge in any other of his usual anxiety-relieving tactics. In the sessions with the therapist, he is encouraged to regress and allow his deepest feelings to dominate his entire being. Mentally and emotionally he again becomes the child he once was, reliving his past and expressing the feelings he was forced to suppress in childhood.

In this regressed state he uses the language of childhood. He cries out for help, or vents in cries and screams the rage he could never before allow to reach consciousness. Now, however, he has with him a part of his adult self that can inject new elements into these recordings of old memories. He is able to digest and complete the unfinished business of the past, freeing his potentiality for growth. In time he becomes capable of achieving voluntary regression, and from that point on he is in large part his own therapist.

But before this stage occurs, it should be pointed out that intense feeling therapy is not the kind of treatment that a therapist can initiate in June then interrupt with a vacation in July. Once a patient's defenses are down they must be kept down, and this is only possible if there is someone to take the therapist's place when he is not available.

At the end of the three-week crash program, the patient enters a group for three sessions per week. These groups, however, are vastly different from those of traditional group therapy. As the patients enter the room they have little to say. Each goes to a different part of the room, lies down, and goes into the voluntary regressed state he has learned to enter in the three-week intensive program. If he has difficulty, as often happens, the therapist helps him. The therapist might ask, "Where are you now?" or simply encourage him to persevere. The patient, having been previously instructed, might answer or remain silent. After roughly two hours he may leave without having said a word to the other patients; or he may remain and join a discussion group to discuss newly emergent insights and childhood memories. Interaction is not encouraged. Occasionally a patient, listening to the others, may experience sudden pain, but instead of reacting to the other patients, he may leave the group and re-enter his regressed state in an effort to discover the feeling that may lead him to old memories and the source of the pain.

I tend to minimize the discussion at the end of these group sessions, since it goes counter to the basic theme of intensity. Discussion involves suppression of feeling for the benefit of group cohesion. Also, it is especially difficult for patients to relate in the group immediately after completing the three-week intensive period.

One outstanding feature of this whole approach is the welcoming of pain and, if the everyday situation permits, allowing it to take over. If this happens, pain inevitably leads to very intense feelings connected with childhood and sometimes to actual memories of the original sources of the pain. The patient has no need of explanations or interpretations from the therapist. He learns from his own innermost feelings.

TREATMENT STAGES

The description of the following stages, first suggested by Irwin Badin, Ph.D., is based upon his own experience in therapy and upon his clinical experience as a therapist. The following constitutes a more detailed analysis of these stages, the essentials of which have also been verified by patients who have successfully completed therapy.

Stage 1. Disarming of Defenses

This stage involves disarming the patient's defense mechanisms. As noted, the basic technique is a three-week intensive period, and it is very effective with individuals who use relationships only in order to satisfy inner needs —for example, seeking love, seeking vindictive triumph for not getting love, and so on. However, for those who tend to keep their interpersonal involvements superficial there is less likelihood that isolation will succeed in increasing tension.

The major therapeutic obstacle during this phase is the patient's fear of feeling—a fear that is often exaggerated. Culturally, the expression of intense emotion is generally discouraged. Screaming and crying are civilized out of us. But our patient is encouraged to let his feelings surface and assume control. They will take him back to the time of their origin, and he will deal with them as though the past were the present. One patient reported his memories during this intensive period as resembling the snatches of film shown for coming attractions in a movie theater. In later primals these bits and pieces of memory were expanded into complete scenes.

Progress during this first stage varies with individual patients. A few never achieve the altered state of consciousness. They cannot externalize what has previously been internalized, and they continue to hate themselves instead of hating the cause of their self-hate. They cannot experience the therapist as anything but an authority figure. They may do their primals in order to gain his favor, but the spurious quality of these primals becomes apparent from the patients' use of adult language and voice, and repetitious mouthings aimed at pleasing the therapist.

For most patients, the first stage begins slowly and then proceeds at an accelerating pace. Getting into the altered state of consciousness is a great strain, rather like climbing part of the way up a hill, then sliding back with fatigue and frustration. But finally one gets to the top; and the rest of the journey is downhill. Here, again, there is variation from patient to patient. Occasionally one will experience this enormous breakthrough with great delight, the most momentous experience of his life; but then, instead of continuing the next day, he may become terrified and want to quit. Yet most patients, once they experience the breakthrough and can connect it with some memories, however fleeting, hunger for it and are able to reachieve it with little assistance from the therapist.

Stage 2. Anger and Sadness

The second stage is marked by the release of pent-up feelings—anger, and occasionally sadness and hurt. These feelings do not emerge from deeper levels but have importance nevertheless. Typically, this stage is characterized by a lashing out. The patient has become aware of his parents' role in containing his feelings, and now he wants revenge.

"I'll kill you," he snarls. "I hate you." Colorful epithets spew out. The patient becomes intent on exacting a retaliatory punishment commensurate with the injury he feels he has suffered. He kicks, punches, and scratches. He wants to tear and break things as he thrashes about.

The sadness and hurt result from the patient's feeling, for the first time, the wrong done to him. He begins to see the futility of his past life and how immersed he has been in the never-ending and hopeless struggle for his parents' love and approval. He oscillates between sadness, a hunger for love, and fury as a result of his deprivation.

Following these two stages, the patient usually experiences three dominant feelings: euphoria, gratitude, and a desire to withdraw from social interaction.

EUPHORIA.   For the first time in his life the patient has a sense of freedom. He has discovered that he can let himself feel without the world crashing down on him. He is highly optimistic, feeling that at some point he will be free of his struggle. The patient is willing to spend as much time as necessary because he feels that he can make it.

GRATITUDE.   The patient is grateful to the therapist who showed the way. The conjunction of this gratitude with optimism regarding the benefits of the therapy go a long way in helping the patient improve.

DESIRE TO WITHDRAW FROM SOCIAL INTERACTION.   After leaving the three-week intensive program, the patient has returned to ordinary life. Because he no longer relies on his old defense mechanisms, he perceives that many relationships served as a symbolic acting-out of his struggle. He has just gained a new sense of freedom—to feel spontaneously —and he is afraid that playing old games might jeopardize this.

Stage 3. Primals Relating to Events of Superficial Importance

Now the patient has many different primals in which he relives some of the crises of his early life, allowing himself to feel the emotions he felt forced to cut off as a child. In essence he is finishing off old, uncompleted scenes, rewriting the early scripts to attain closure. While a few of these scenes were of crucial importance to the patient, many of them were not, and reliving them a few times resolves his residual anxiety regarding them. As he eliminates these less important episodes, he begins to concentrate on those which were crucial, the fourth stage of the primal process.

Stage 4. Primals Relating to Crucial Episodes

In this stage most of the work gets done. The patient has zeroed in on several key episodes of varying importance. Each of them may have been accompanied by great pain, never previously acknowledged. Each may be very complex, suffused with a number of emotions which were repressed at the time. Further, a particular scene may epitomize the child's struggle and pain.

These key episodes are continually re-experienced; the aim is to finish each scene, to feel the emotions that were denied consciousness at the time the episode took place. The number of returns to a particular episode depends upon several factors. One is the amount of pain involved in experiencing the previously repressed emotions. In reliving a scene involving parental rejection, for example, the patient feels intense anger and rage—emotions that stimulate severe guilt. One patient, after taking sadistic delight in "killing" her mother, had fantasies of cutting off her own hands. Such a patient may allow herself to feel these intense emotions only in gradual stages.

The patient is now dealing with extremely crucial material. The successful completion of these scenes will be the key that unlocks his authentic self. This fourth stage takes longer than any of the others; some patients remain in it for more than a year.

This stage is probably the most puzzling to the therapist; a patient continually repeats the same scene, apparently with no progress. Actually the patient is slowly coming to terms with his deepest emotions, those that he has struggled over an entire lifetime not to feel.

In stages 3 and 4, the patient reports a feeling of being lost, or disconnected from himself—a terribly uncomfortable sensation. The patient can no longer rely on his defenses to block feelings, and when they surface it is not always possible for him to stop where he is and have a primal. In such circumstances, tension builds very rapidly, and the only way left for the patient to deal with it is to disconnect himself from his mind and body in fear of slipping back into his old false self. He becomes an observer of himself, perceiving himself as a split-off object. In addition, the patient is now beginning to become more "real." He begins to experience spontaneous feelings that are somewhat frightening. He proceeds cautiously to this new self, but even a cautious pace arouses anxiety.

The therapist now becomes a supportive figure rather than the strict overseer he was at the start, supporting more constructive feelings and behavior.

The intensity and duration of disconnected feeling varies from patient to patient. The most crucial factor is the amount of fear associated with being real. A patient who believes that being real has terrible consequences is the one most likely to get stuck, caught in a double-avoidance conflict. He does not wish to return to his old neurotic games, nor could he if he wanted to; yet he is uncomfortable with being a new person. In extreme cases, these factors may prevent him from succeeding at all. However, a therapist's warmth can ease these fears and make the transitions smoother.

Stage 5. Synthesis

This stage begins when the patient is able to feel again the honest, deep openness he had for his parents before he experienced their rejection. He feels the young child's openness, but he also experiences the opposite. There is a feeling of terrible void as he realizes that his beautiful openness to life was crushed. He sees how he had to warp himself in order to get love.

The patient now experiences a great deal of deep sadness, feeling it throughout his entire body. In addition, there is anger—but a deeper anger than the emotion felt in the second stage. The earlier anger was characterized by a lashing out, but now the patient knows that killing or beating his parents will not bring the reciprocated love he so badly wanted. The anger he feels now does not need vengeance to satisfy it. He is angry at his parents for what they did, but he knows the hopelessness of trying to make them pay for, or even understand, his feeling.

As all this comes to the surface, the patient can feel, for the first time, the entire nature of his struggle. He now understands the myriad contradictory feelings that have surfaced in his primaling. He can feel what it was like to give an open, innocent love and not have it returned for its own sake. He can truly understand, at a feeling level, his ambivalence toward his parents as well as the nature of his neurotic adjustment. This stage is truly one of synthesis on a feeling level.

Now he settles into primals that become a reliving of the point at which the split took place, which he experienced in earlier primals only in transitory flashes.

Stage 6. The Authentic Self

The patient experiences a reduction of the sensation of being lost and disconnected. Having felt the hopelessness of his struggle and the futility of his neurotic adjustments, he can now attempt to behave in more authentic ways without fear of losing his parents' love. He becomes less an observer of himself. He feels the needs of his real self and wants them satisfied.

At the same time, the patient may still have a tendency to be overwhelmed by feelings in social settings. However, as the store of repressed emotions becomes fully connected to old experiences, these social anxieties diminish.

The patient continues to primal. Usually the primals center around the split, but occasionally the patient will begin to primal about some other experience, as in stage 4. All of the previously stray feelings are now connected to their source—the split. Ultimately the amount of primaling decreases, both because there is less unfinished business from the past and because the patient's life is now lived in more authentic terms. His life becomes truly his own.

PATIENT TYPES

Patients who are successful in therapy go through the above stages. They are the ones who need the therapist less and less as time goes on. They have no need to report their progress to the therapist and often feel no need for the talk sessions. While they recognize the great neurosis of the outer world they do not necessarily withdraw from it; indeed, they are able to play the necessary games and roles when required to. The real successes do not need access to a primal community, even though they may prefer relating to others who have had similar experiences. They are able to recognize inappropriate feelings in the present, resist the temptation to act out or seek other relief from the pain, bide their time until they have an opportunity to go into a primal, and then connect with some hurt in the past.

On the other hand, a number of patients do not go through the six stages to real autonomy. Their hunger for connectedness to a parent is too strong, and they continue to make demands upon the therapist for time and attention. These individuals, while making considerable progress, need a person to cling to. They seek a primal community —which they believe is the ultimate answer—because they cannot free themselves of their morbid dependence. In this "community" they will always find someone to relate to. They may state that they are comfortable with others who are familiar with this new therapy and who are in the same boat; but they really want to sustain the false hope of finding a mommy. For these patients, the therapist has to tread a thin line. If their dependency needs are not satisfied to some extent, they withdraw; and if they are satisfied, there is a danger of morbid dependency.

Another group of patients go only part of the way because of the intense terror they experience in regression. For these patients the experience is a "death primal," and they need the presence of a therapist. In this state, some have enormous fear of not being able to breathe. Others are jumpy, easily startled at any sudden sound or touch. In this group are the many patients whose bodies have become literally distorted by the conflict, and they invariably experience physical pain as the body attempts to untwist itself in the healing process. They make great progress but never seem to go all the way. Conversely, patients who do well are able to be largely independent. They have developed the capacity not to run away from pain but to remain with it and, when necessary, enter the regressed state to discharge tensions and to connect with early sources.

Conclusions

I do not claim, as Janov (1970) does, that my intense feeling therapy achieves 90 per cent "cures." And while I question whether Janov's claim is justified, he nevertheless does focus upon two great flaws in present practice.

One flaw is the fifty-minute hour, which originated in order to fit the treatment of the patient to the convenience of the therapist. Neurosis is a disease of feelings, and feelings must be available if changes are to occur. In the three-week crash program of intense feeling therapy, the attempt is made to undermine defenses against feelings and to keep these defenses down—in essence, to get feelings flowing. This occurs by concentrating upon nothing but therapy for three weeks, with the patient kept in isolation except for sessions with the therapist. With the fifty-minute hour, however, the patient is somehow supposed to switch on feelings when the hour begins and then, when time is up, to switch them off and return to his usual routine.

The second great flaw concerns the possibility of a malignant transference. In intense feeling therapy, transference is minimized by having the patient talk to himself (internalized parental figures), thereby becoming his own therapist, and by having him join a group after the three-week crash program ends.

Freud was on the brink of discovering the importance of his patients' full expression of their most primitive feelings. However, the painful feelings expressed by his patients were apparently too overwhelming for Freud, and he resorted to the couch to avoid facing patients as he grappled with the intensity of the emotional outpouring. His therapy was ultimately diverted from a feeling one to a talking one, with the adult patient talking about the child within him as if the child were a third person. With this, the patient's feelings now flowed toward Freud—the process called transference. Freud emphasized the need to analyze this transference as part of the therapeutic process, and all analysts are aware of how difficult this process is. All patients who have been in therapy continue to have profound feelings for the therapist as a surrogate parent.

Another flaw is that orthodox Freudians tend to focus upon the patient's oedipal stage, because at this stage language exists. The pre-oedipal stage, when the patient has no language at his command, is beyond the reach of analysis. The importance of the pre-oedipal years was not fully recognized by Freud. Recently, the work of Fairbairn (1952) and Guntrip (1964, 1968) points to these years as most important, but, because of the continued reliance upon adult language, no effective therapy has evolved.

The Freudians recognize the earlier, pre-oedipal trauma, but since the therapeutic approach is too verbal they have no way of dealing with this period. The same might be said of Horney and Sullivan, who dealt more with defenses that developed in the post-oedipal period. On the other hand, the noninsight therapies disregard the defenses and concentrate on coping in the here and now, developing fully whatever assets are discoverable.

Another great distinction between intense feeling therapy and other modalities is that in the former there is an emphasis upon a therapeutic acting-in, whereas in the others there is mostly a defensive acting-out. In the regressed state the patient lives the past as a child and talks to ghosts of the past in the present tense. He is projecting on an imaginary screen what was introjected early in life. It is like a dream or a play in which the patient is the author, producer, actors, director, even scenery. The harmful introjects are then experienced outside him, and he can allow the emergence of hitherto suppressed and repressed emotions. Only now is he able to change the script. He can behave and feel in entirely new ways. He can even alter the characters and imagine what a good parent might have given him, and then become a good parent to himself.

In the traditional psychotherapeutic dyad or group the patient cannot help but act out the internal conflicts, and in this way transference occurs. In acting out he has to share the stage with others who are beyond his control. He will try to mold the others—if he does not retreat altogether—into figures from the past in order to feel at home. And acting out merely perpetuates the neurosis.

After more than four years of great success with this new therapy, I nevertheless see certain limitations. One criticism of Janov is that he regards character structure as involving only one feeling-axis—the strength-weakness axis. This point of view is an outgrowth of our times, because it is necessary to have strength to be alone and not feel the loneliness which is inevitable in this society. In today's world there is no tribe, there is little family, there is almost nothing to belong to. In addition, the scene changes from day to day, so that rootedness is impossible. It is increasingly difficult for an individual to feel any responsibility for the welfare of others. Each person must resort to the strength in himself.

Janov (1970) describes the post-primal patients as being free of tension, with much less sex drive or social drive. They do not sound like life-loving people with a feeling of responsibility to others or to society. Further, they seem contemptuous of others who have not been through primal therapy.

Janov is disappointed because he discovers that his patients become apolitical. In a sense he overcures them, so that the healthy dependency and need for others disappears with the resolution of the neurotic dependency. The individual is still left with a void, even though he is free of tension. It is of interest that four of Janov's therapists, after some disagreements with him about theory and treatment, left him to form their own group—the Center for Feeling Therapy, in California. It seems to me that they sensed Janov's neglect of this need to belong, and they superimposed conventional group meetings upon the rest of Janov's program.

Another difficulty I find is that there are some individuals who make the new therapy into a way of life. They keep talking about how they are "getting there," but from all I can see they tend to stay at the same level.

Lately, I have begun to consider two new possibilities for group work. The first is to use the group situation, with which we are all familiar, as a trial for new patients to see if they are regression-prone. Some patients may be able to act out and to see the irrationality of the acting out, but not to feel the source in the past. Some are so locked in with their acting out, their search for a love object, or vindictive behavior, that it is almost impossible for them to suspend their critical faculties and regress to childhood. Obviously such patients are not suited for intense feeling therapy.

A second possibility for group work may be with patients of an entirely different type—those who are well along in intense feeling therapy. Such patients might use a variety of encounter techniques to explore new avenues of behavior and feeling. Perhaps the group would provide a good testing ground to assess changes and uncover residual defensiveness.

There is no question in my mind that the effectiveness of intense feeling therapy will eventually be established. For therapists who must remain in their present setting I have some suggestions.

1. Have the patient come half an hour early, remaining in the waiting room to ruminate about the past and bring up feelings. Also, have the patient remain in the waiting room after the session in order to digest what happened.

2. Encourage more activity in the session, but always attempt to make feeling connections with the past. Let the patient's feelings lead the way.

3. Encourage the same activity in group work, especially when feelings are triggered by neurotic interactions. Again, have each patient talk in the present tense to the ghosts of the past.

4. In the group sessions, encourage patients to re-enact the neurotic interactions to see whether the script changes with the new insights.

In conclusion, I anticipate that more regression will be encouraged by therapists and that this regression will be extremely beneficial for those patients who function relatively well and who at the same time are open to feelings. Each therapist will eventually be confronted with the difficult decision of whether or not to put patients through the crash program. If the therapist experiences the treatment himself, the decision will be much easier for him to make.

chapter 6

EMOTIONAL FLOODING: A TECHNIQUE IN SENSORY HYPNOANALYSIS

Milton V. Kline, Ed.D.

The development of a therapeutic approach emphasizing the use of sensory order within an analytic framework has been described earlier as sensory hypnoanalysis (Kline 1966). As an experimental treatment approach, it has been designed to expand sensory experience, at first with a restriction of verbal output accompanied by the intensification of visual imagery as an intermediate experiential involvement between amplification of sensory response and verbalization.

To a considerable extent, the techniques described within the framework of sensory hypnoanalysis have been strongly influenced by the recognition of the importance of the sensory order in relation to psychodynamics and the body language of communication in emotional disorders and psychosomatic disturbances. In addition, it has been recognized that within the hypnotic process, the role of sensory-motor imagery activity assumes a level of accessibility that is frequently not encountered in therapeutic settings where hypnosis is not employed. Earlier work by Kline (1952a, 1953a) and Schneck (1950, 1952) had stimulated interest in the spontaneous arousal of sensory responses during hypnosis and their management in psychotherapy.

This was particularly noticed in connection with the induction of hypnosis and the subjective reports that patients frequently made of the presence of sensory experience and its direct relationship to body-image components, often with direct and meaningful linkage to pertinent aspects of the patient's memory, perceptual process, associative function, and focal symptom development (Kline 1953 b, 1967). Kline confirmed the importance of the sensory order in connection with its use as an induction procedure, particularly in refractory subjects, and in the ability to utilize sensory and imagery components in both the amplification and deepening of the hypnotic state (1952b, 1953a, 1963). Particularly evident have been those neuropsychological reactions which, aroused by sensory experience, are reflected in alterations in time-space percepts. It is also evident that such changes often coincide with the rapidly emerging transference phenomenon that can become an integral part of the developing hypnotic process and can lend itself not only to spontaneous experiential involvement but also to the productive utilization of what has been described as a rapid and spontaneous regression. This is characterized by increasing use of primary process and reorganization of perceptual and sensory mechanisms (Kline 1953c).

Sensory-imagery techniques in hypnotherapy were originally reported in connection with the successful treatment of benign paroxysmal peritonitis (Kline 1954), psoriasis, and neurodermatitis (Kline 1960). Since that time, modifications of this treatment procedure have been

reported in connection with a wide range of neurotic characterologic and psychophysiological disorders (Kline 1952
b, 1967). Ament and Milgrom (1967) have recently reported on its incorporation in the successful treatment of
pruritus with cutaneous lesions in chronic myelogenous
leukemia.

The original introduction of hypnoplasty by Meares
(1960) and its provocative relationship to the productively
regressive development of the hypnotic process was a further development in the identification of the importance of
hypnosis and of the fundamental changes in communication that were possible within the hypnotic relationship.
Finally, the modifications and developments by Raginsky
(1962, 1967) of his therapeutic system and approach
known as sensory hypnoplasty have served as a clinical and
conceptual basis for some of the approaches, techniques,
and mechanisms employed within psychotherapy structured as sensory hypnoanalysis. As described by Raginsky
(1962), sensory hypnoplasty is a technique in which the
hypnotized patient models plasticine to which various sensory stimuli have been added to stimulate basic memories,
associations, and conflicts. This allows the patient to give
plastic expression to repressed and suppressed material;
this is then followed by verbalization of the conflicts. Thus,
the investigative and therapeutic processes are initiated
exceptionally quickly and intensified markedly. The conflicts are expressed first in plastic symbols, which in essence
means sensory construction, and then after a time gap,
verbalized. Raginsky (1967) has also reported the rapid
regression to oral and anal levels through the use of sensory hypnoplasty.

This is consistent with the author's observations of the
rapidity with which a variety of regressive mechanisms are
stimulated through the use of sensory procedures in hypnosis and become expressed both through bodily reactions

and behavioral output representative of various stages of ego development, particularly emphasizing oral, anal, and phallic levels (Kline 1953c, 1963, 1967).

Sensory hypnoanalysis as a systematic approach in psychotherapy begins with the patient's immediate focus upon his own sensory awareness directed primarily by those reactions which he himself experiences, beginning with the induction of hypnosis. Spontaneous reactions are then used to elaborate upon the initial stages. The patient is instructed at first not to verbalize what is experienced during the hypnotic session itself but simply to permit the sensory directed experiences to unfold and develop in whatever manner they wish to.

Following one or two such nonverbal sessions, the patient learns to permit elements of sensory experience to become organized into behavioral units that involve sensations, imagery, memory, and, frequently, associative activity. He knows at what point to begin to verbalize and to relate his verbalizations to personal experiences, conflicts, and therapeutic goals. The therapist serves primarily to initiate and, at times, comment upon some of the material that may be verbalized and, as organized responses are presented, to make clinical interpretations at appropriate times. It has been found that the role of clinical interpretation in sensory hypnoanalysis is an extremely potent device, even more so than in nonhypnotic psychoanalytic therapy, and serves the dual purposes of interpretation as an analytic process as well as an indirect suggestive device within the hypnotic process.

For selected patients with whom intensive hypnoanalytic procedures are being employed, a separate room has, at times, been set aside to which the patient retires following a hypnoanalytic session. In this room are all of the facilities necessary for communicating in whatever form the patient may wish. There are materials for sculpting with clay, including plasticine; materials for drawing, painting, writing; and a couch upon which to relax or to sleep and dream.

It has been found that the hours following such therapeutic sessions have frequently been important periods for the patient to organize and integrate many of his reactions that occurred during the treatment session. In other instances, patients will find the drive and need to express themselves later in the day, frequently in the evening when the day's work has been completed. There is no formal characteristic as to the time, manner, or procedure of communication, and it occurs very much in keeping with the needs of the patient. At times it will follow a number of sessions consecutively; at other times, there may be gaps or periods during which nothing additional is communicated. It would appear that these gaps are periods during which there was an integrating process going on, and something like a plateau in the learning process is encountered, with communication occurring at some later point.

As a specialized form of hypnoanalysis, it has been found that this approach has been most effective in dealing with regressive aspects of characterological disorders, especially in patients who present psychosomatic symptoms. Particular value has been found in using this selected approach with patients who have had a good deal of verbal analytic psychotherapy previously but for whom therapeutic results have been minimal and conflict behavior and symptoms persistent. As such, it has been found that obsessive-compulsive patients, those displaying depressive features as well as borderline schizophrenic reactions, have been especially responsive to this approach.

Sensory hypnoanalysis has been found to rapidly facilitate abreactive experiences, spontaneous age regressions, the intensification and frequency of nocturnal dreaming, and the spontaneous ventilating of rapidly emerging feelings directly bound in with conflict phenomena. It has thus been possible to work at a sensory and analytic level simultaneously, and to utilize, on an interrelated basis, hypnotic and analytic techniques very rapidly in a treatment situation which without the use of hypnosis might not be accessible for a long time—or, in many instances, not at all (Kine 1960, 1963, 1967).

Frequently the material produced through a sensory hypnoanalysis session and the experiences that follow lend themselves best to discussion and evaluation in a waking psychotherapy session. Thus, it occurs frequently that the use of hypnoanalysis will incorporate sessions during which no hypnosis may be used, depending upon the timing and the significance of the emerging material and patient response.

Induction is usually initiated through the use of either a direct or indirect sensory-imagery technique. The procedure for this type of induction has been described earlier (Kline 1953a), and the approach in sensory hypnoanalysis involves essentially this method with a number of clinical modifications based upon the nature of patient response. Following the initial session, the patient is asked to describe what he has subjectively experienced, and the nature of his own sensory-imagery reactions are used in subsequent sessions to structure the treatment plan. This initial induction period serves as both a diagnostic and projective vehicle for shaping the treatment plan of sensory hypnoanalysis.

The visual-imagery technique for induction and diagnostic evaluation is as follows:

1. In the waking state, with eyes open, each subject is asked to visualize in his mind's eye certain familiar objects. In order, these are: (1) a house, (2) a tree, (3) a person, and (4) an animal. This is continued until each stimulus has been achieved.

2. Following image formation in the waking state, each patient is told, "Close your eyes and in your mind's eye visualize yourself as you are here; sitting in the chair (or lying on the couch) except that the image of yourself has his (her) eyes open."

3. At this point, the patient is told to concentrate on the image; he is informed that all the therapist's comments will be directed toward the patient's image and not toward the subject.

4. A simple visual fixation technique, as described, is used and related to the eye closure of the image. Close clinical observation of the subject will reveal subtle response patterns indicating the associative effect upon him directly. The subject can be asked to confirm eye closure in the image, though often his own straining to raise his eyebrows will reveal the situation. Following eye closure in the image, suggestions for deepening the trance are given in the usual manner.

5. The next step involves moving directly into the induction relationship with the patient. This may be done by saying, "Now you are feeling just like the image, going deeper and deeper asleep (or an equated word), and the image is disappearing." Within a few minutes, depending on the patient's personality, you will have obtained a light to medium hypnotic trance. Further depth may be secured in the usual manner, but the patient is now ready for hypnotherapeutic work.

The total elapsed time of this induction technique has averaged ten minutes. Where there is deviation, it tends to be a shorter rather than a longer time.

With projective techniques and hypnotic visual imagery, these methods can, in a reasonably brief period of time, reveal a great deal of information with respect to a patient's characterologic structure and ego functioning.

The techniques of visual-imagery induction can be combined with projective testing, and the extent to which the light hypnotic state increases patient productivity becomes very apparent.

Data from one clinical case are presented to illustrate the psychodiagnostic value of even very light hypnotic states. The use of modified versions of the House-Tree-Person (H-T-P) and Thematic Apperception Tests are described in connection with hypnodiagnosis and visual imagery in a refractory patient.

In clinical practice it has been found that this technique is particularly well suited for use in connection with projective psychological testing. Projective hypnodiagnostic testing in itself is a rapidly expanding technique which, in recent years, has been increasingly described in the literature. Although this chapter does not deal with either the theoretical rationale or technical interpretation methods for projective tests and hypnosis, it should be noted that a series of clinical and experimental studies in this general area reveal the following trends for a large percentage of patients so tested:

1. With hypnosis, there is a general overall increase in psychologic productivity.

2. There is usually fuller imagery activity.

3. Sensory and motor correlates of the imagery often become involved in the hypnotic visualization response though not in the waking response.

4. Hypnotic responses tend to incorporate aspects of transference activity on a more active level.

The visual-imagery technique fits into a projective hypnodiagnostic approach very easily, because it can be arrived at indirectly—without using the term "hypnosis," if its omission is necessary—and is consistent with a diagnostic orientation within which the interview is perceived by the patient as being decidedly patient-centered. Such an expectation of productivity by the patient makes for easy acceptance of this technique.

With a visual-imagery induction technique, the H-T-P visualizations are first obtained in the waking state as part of the actual induction. Then, after hypnosis has been achieved, the visualizations are obtained again. The differences between the two sets of visualizations, as well as their actual content, add to the meaning of the projections. Controlled studies with repeated waking series have failed to elucidate the differences and psychodynamic reflections found in the combined waking-hypnotic administration.

CASE MATERIAL

A twenty-six-year-old married woman was referred for psychotherapy because of periodic cycles of rather intense depression and a variety of skin and respiratory allergies that her physicians felt were on a psychosomatic basis. During the first session, it appeared that the patient was rather coarctated with respect to important life history productivity and was also refractory to hypnosis with a variety of induction techniques. In the second interview, the visual-imagery induction technique was used, and a light hypnotic state resulted. Following are the H-T-P visualizations in the waking and hypnotic states:

(*Waking*) HOUSE: This is a pretty house. Right near it there is a rose arbor which is very nice to sit under and relax near. It has a pretty cobblestone path and it's a cute house. It has flowers and is generally associated with good things and good weather and prosperity.

(*Hypnosis*) HOUSE: This is a witch's house. It's very old and musty and very bad. It's a very unhappy house, and it keeps people locked inside. But in the meanwhile it has a lot of windows so that people can look inside and criticize you. Everything around the house is dead. There's only rocks and a dead tree and a cold moon. The person who drew this is very unhappy because there is nothing loving around her but everything is dead and nobody cares for her.

(*Waking*) TREE: I associate this tree with myself. It's —ah—it's what I hope to—ah—it's big because I—I'm going to try to—ah—it has no leaves, yet I associate it with acquiring a certain—certain amount of physical attractiveness and I feel that by trying hard, an—and putting my mind to it that the leaves that are missing on this tree will eventually, you know, materialize. I associate the size of the tree with myself. Actually, I feel that I'm much too short and very—and heavy for my size and I wish I could be tall and yet I feel that by working at it—an—and planning and doing other things that eventually my size won't be important any more.

(*Hypnosis*) TREE: This tree is really a person. The person is very short and is not good-looking, and the tree has no beautiful leaves or anything nice, and the roots try to go way down deep to find something to make it grow beautiful and happy, but there's nothing there.

(*Waking*) PERSON (*female*):   Here again I associate myself with it. It is an endeavor to be glamorous and attractive and sophisticated and acting older, and I think that's about all.

(*Hypnosis*) PERSON (*female*):   This is me going to school. I am not pretty. I dress in funny clothes. I try hard to please people around me. That's why I'm carrying an apple, and I try very hard to be smart so people will like me because I'm smart.

(*Waking*) PERSON (*male*): I feel that I've pictured here a man who is—ah—sophisticated to a certain degree—and —yet compatibly good-looking and gentle, who'd learn social obligations and little duties and things like that. I consider that important. I don't like a man who is particularly coarse in any way.

(*Hypnosis*) PERSON (*male*): This is a nice, good-looking fellow who goes to school. I like him very much and I think he likes me, but I am very shy, and whenever I see him looking at me I make believe I don't see him, but then again maybe I'm only imagining that he looks at me and he really isn't, because if he is how do I know he's not laughing at me, because he's so big and popular and everything and I'm not.

Following this, the patient was given, in the waking state, several Thematic Apperception cards with the following administrative modifications: "I would like you to look at this card for one minute. I will time you. When the time is up, I will say 'close your eyes.' Then I would like you to visualize in your mind the picture you just saw and to tell me what it is about."

Following this, the cards were administered in the same manner in the hypnotic state. Modifications of these directions can easily be made to fit any particular situation both with respect to patient and test. Following are some of the waking and hypnotic TAT visualizations:

(*Waking*) CARD I: Well, I feel that this boy is studying the violin and that he loves it. He feels that someday he's going to be a great violinist, and I also think that perhaps his father or grandfather was a violinist and this is one of the reasons why he wishes to follow in their footsteps.

(*Hypnosis*) CARD 1: This little boy is looking at a violin, and he doesn't like the violin. He's not allowed to play it because no one else in his house ever knew how to play the violin, and they won't let him play it because they don't know any better, because they're ignorant, so he wants to smash the violin.

(*Waking*) CARD 12M: The old man is jealous of the young boy who is sleeping, and he has an impulse to hit the face of the young boy. He wants to push it in. However, it is very possible that the young boy will wake up and avert the old man's hand.

(*Hypnosis*) CARD 12M: This young boy is either dead or dying, and the old man is saying good-bye, and he feels very angry with the world that this young boy, who is possibly his son, has died, and yet in his hand there is a certain amount of lovingness, too, and he is going to place his hand on the boy's shoulder and perhaps kiss him good-bye.

(*Waking*) CARD 14:   This young man is looking out the window at stars. He is on the top floor of a tenement, and he has climbed up to the top, and he is very pleased by what he sees, and he hopes that the moon will come out.

(*Hypnosis*) CARD 14:   This fellow is on the top or near the top of a building. He is going to jump out the window and fly away. Yes, he's going to fly; he's going to fly way, way, way up, and when he sees a cloud he's going to dive through it. When he sees the moon he's going to try to reach it, and I only hope that he doesn't land in red mud.

Thus, in addition to facilitating a rapid though light state of hypnosis in otherwise relatively refractory subjects, the visual-imagery induction technique lends itself particularly well to projective hypnodiagnosis. With competent clinical management, it helps to establish a hypno-therapeutic or hypnoanalytic treatment approach early in therapy and to assist in the diagnostic elucidation of unconscious ideation and affect as well as the way in which the patient tends to defend against them. In appropriate cases, it can become both an effective technique in relation to treatment goals and an efficient device with respect to treatment time.

Therapeutic Illustration:

CASE A.   A thirty-seven-year-old woman was referred by her internist with a presenting history of hysterical dysphonia and a paralysis of the right hand when it was necessary for her to write. Writing was an important part of her professional work. The patient had had two years of prior psychotherapy, during which time there had been no symptomatic improvement. It is interesting to note that the hand involved in the paralysis during writing was the same hand that the patient used most effectively in playing tennis regularly.

Initial sensory hypnoanalysis used hypnotic induction to focus upon the hand, after conceptualization of total bodily awareness. The patient was told that she would be able to visualize the hand and that she would be able to "feel every sensation in the hand." Intensification of these sensations produced an expression of great agitation followed by hysterical sobbing, the placing of the right thumb in the mouth, and a series of sucking movements which continued uninterrupted for some thirty minutes. Following this, the patient became calm, at ease, and finally removed her thumb from her mouth and in a somewhat childish voice said, "I suppose it is impossible to either talk or write when your thumb is in your mouth, isn't it?" Following this session the patient made use of the adjoining room, at first simply to relax, then to spontaneously write out in great detail a variety of early recollections that could never be expressed verbally and that became symbolized in almost homicidal impulses to strike out.

During the following sessions, the patient continued to use her sensory experiences to elaborate many of these long-repressed and little-understood feelings and to link them up with the secondary gains resulting from her symptoms. The dysphonia spontaneously improved within three sessions, and from the first session the patient would produce longhand notations that she left after each treatment session. Writing continued to improve, and all sensations of pain and discomfort in the right hand disappeared within a period of several weeks.

CASE B.   A twenty-one-year-old male, discharged from military service as the result of a psychiatric hospitalization and emerging homosexuality, described himself as extremely depressed, impotent, and suicidal. Until his entry into military service, he had lived with his parents but had not spoken one word to his father for seven years. With an IQ of 135, he had nevertheless held only menial jobs following graduation from high school, and while he presented an outward appearance of extreme passivity, infantilism, and signs of depersonalization, there was no recognition of any inner range or bound-up drive potential.

The following sensory hypnoanalytic session began with instructions to visualize the penis and testicles and to "feel the body," particularly the genital area, which, as he described the sensations, gave rise to increasing agitated anxiety and the following spontaneous verbalization:

> I see my father. He looks like a monster. Evil and cunning.
> His eyes are wicked and exciting. He starts to tear my balls
> off when I try to be friendly to him. He seems wild and crazy.
> I am afraid that he is going to hurt me very much.

In reality, the father was described as being extremely dull, stupid, ineffectual, and not in any way a source of anxiety. During the course of this hypnoanalytic session, the patient shivered and was in extreme panic.

Following the session, by himself, in the adjoining treatment room, the patient wrote:

> To love someone who loves not,
> To wait for someone who waits not,
> To go to someone who waits not,
> This is my father.

The patient then wrote that he recalled a dream from very early childhood before he went to school, and that he used to have this dream repeatedly night after night. The dream involved his being in the woods with his mother. The mother would take the patient into a cave and tell him that she would meet him at the other end a little later. In the cave, the patient would meet a clown who allowed the patient to go through the cave. He was all alone with the clown, and he was terrified.

Later, he described the fact that as a child he had thought of clowns not as happy, pleasant people, but as mean and sneaky. He was terrified of them. He also said, "That's why I wanted to be a girl. It was safer, freer. I could dance around and not be vulnerable. Then the clowns might like me, like my father liked my sister."

CASE C. A twenty-seven-year-old married woman was seen at the recommendation of her physician and priest. She was severely depressed, increasingly dependent upon alcohol, and involved in promiscuous sexual behavior. During two initial consultations, she found it almost physically impossible to talk and could not even verbalize simple replies to direct questions.

The third session involved hypnosis with sensory imagery of the body while lying on the couch. The patient was told that she would be able to visualize the body and "sense" what was going on within it. No verbalization took place during the actual hypnosis. Following the session, the patient wrote the following report.

> A demon dwells within me, casting shadows upon my days, destroying any hope to be, relentlessly gnawing its prey. Day and night it torments, tortures; like a cancer rotting to the bone. It will not leave me alone, not a minute, not a second. Seeping through all my veins, it paralyzes, terrorizes to unfathomable depths. A veritable hell lies buried in this putrid piece of humanity, brutally destroying everything it nears,

spreading vengeance, hate, hurt, haunting all it reaches. I could tear at the flesh that houses this monster called me, so ugly and hateful an object it is; not worth a damn to anyone, anything. It should be mutilated, smashed to pieces, thrown to hungry wolves before it permeates to greater lengths, before its vileness taints another.

Frightening feelings are these—compelling, lurking all the time, very close at hand. A pitiable state to be in, to loath so much as to reach this degree and intensity of self-hate; to want to inflict such pain and horror because there seems no other answer. No place to put yourself, no joy to feel, no satisfaction obtained. Nothing to hope for, to live for, constant frustration, turmoil, growing by leaps and bounds, the omega of futility and fruitlessness.

After four sessions of sensory hypnoanalysis, she wrote this poem.

Warmth pervades the atmosphere
Someone to talk with beckons as you near.
The eyes you watch, serene and fine
You know will treat you oh so kind
The voice you hear sincere and true
You know will open your heart anew.

No need to pretend
No need to amend
For now you do not have to flee
The hurt you have felt
The torment once hidden
The tears, the fears, repressed for years.

Flow steadily thru—
Until you can find
The self lost to you
Who you never knew.

The above material reflects the verbal and imagery activity stemming from and interlocking with sensory functioning in the hypnoanalytic treatment situation. It leads to productive use of the therapeutic interaction and the transference relationship. Spontaneous material serves to maintain the momentum of the treatment process and to be directly related at times to very rapid therapeutic progress both symptomatically and in a more fundamental characterologic sense.

DISCUSSION

Sensory hypnoanalysis, originally developed as an experimental form of analytic pscyhotherapy for patients who were unresponsive in previous treatment situations, has been influenced by the primacy of sensory functioning in the hypnotic process and its relationship to the productive role of regression in dynamic psychotherapy. The contributions of Meares (1960) and Raginsky (1962, 1967) in the evolvement of hypnoplasty and sensory hypnoplasty have influenced many of the procedures and clinical constructs of sensory hypnoanalysis. The importance of the sensory order has long been recognized as a vital element in the hypnotic process and its incorporation into hypnoanalysis in the form described here has permitted rapid and gratifying therapeutic results, particularly with patients with psychophysiologic disorders, obsessive-compulsive features, and characterologic problems, generally unresponsive to a verbally oriented psychotherapy.

Emotional flooding with hypnosis consists of the development of focal behavioral orientations and the intensification of sensory, motor, and imagery components of the patient's perceptual apparatus. The resulting behavior brings about regressive and abreactive elements—some nonverbal and others sensory in nature—which later become lexical in expression.

In its broadest sense, emotional flooding with hypnosis produces abreactive behavior on a continuum from "silent" to "explosive," and from nonverbal imagery intensification to lexical expression.

The technique of abreaction that has been used in emotive therapy can be described as the hypnotic method for the induction of emotional stress. Abreaction as a term originates in the theater (Aristotle) and permits the patient to act out and revivify as well as discharge meaningful memory and correlated behavioral experiences. Abreaction originated as a therapeutic device alone, and while it has been insufficient very often to produce lasting effects in terms of the treatment of neurotic or psychotic disturbances, it nevertheless, has had a significant role in the history of psychotherapy and continues to be important.

Shorvon and Sargent describe an abreaction as a "process of reviving the memory of a repressed, unpleasant experience and expressing, in speech and action, the emotions related to it, thereby relieving the personality of its importance" (1947). The emphasis in this definition is clearly on the release of the emotions.

Clinicians and therapists who have had considerable experience with abreactions are familiar with the fact that the discharge of released emotions is usually followed by a state of exhaustion in which the patient shows a loss of muscle tone and is quiet. The quietness produces a degree of relaxation that is frequently so great as to have not only momentary but lasting therapeutic value for a varying period of time. Sargent (1957) compares this state of exhaustion to the transmarginal inhibition of Pavlov, in which dogs, following an emotional trauma, lose the previously acquired conditioned reflexes or show a complete reversal of conditioned reaction.

Gelhorn and Loofbourrow (1963) suggest that the physiologic processes underlying the excitatory abreaction are an intensive, hypothalamic-cortical discharge followed by a period of lessened cortico-hypothalamic-cortical relations. The severe hypothalamic-cortical discharge due to extreme excitation is induced by encouraging the patient to relive the traumatic experience. The subsequent reduction of the hypothalamic-cortical discharge is attributed to excessive adrenomedullary secretion, which has been shown to depress the sympathetic division of the hypothalamus; and possibly also to an exhaustion of the hyperreactive division of the hypothalamus. The therapeutic usefulness of the abreaction would appear to depend on whether maximal excitation followed by exhaustion is attained. Clinical experience with continuous abreactive experiences has been demonstrated to markedly relieve a number of pathological symptoms unresponsive to a single abreaction (Kline 1967).

It cannot be overemphasized that many abreactive responses, especially those "silent" in nature and initially expressed as imagery, must then be transformed into lexical organization.

Hypnosis involves the activation of strong transference phenomena between hypnotist and patient or subject, and even within the confines of investigational procedures, the therapeutic meaningfulness of the hypnotic relationship has been repeatedly observed and reported. Thus, within the transference-relaxation aspect of the hypnotic process, there is at the same time induced abreaction that can produce therapeutic value due to its discharge-exhaustion syndrome and, at the same time, involve the subjects in a process of desensitization.

Emotional flooding with hypnosis can be maintained for long periods of time and easily reinforced through self-hypnosis. The use of hypnosis for prolonged stress reduction, the reinforcement of homeostasis through self-hypnosis, and the alteration of sensory and perceptual mechanisms can, in selected patients, yield therapeutic results that had not previously been possible for them (Kline 1963, 1965, 1969).

O'Connell and Orne (1968) suggest that some kind of

"central relaxation" is involved, not simply muscular relaxation, since electrodermal activity, as they describe it, is not muscular in origin but rather autonomic. This is not unrelated to our polygraphic observations in the last several years. Patients during prolonged hypnotic relaxation reveal a persistence of relaxation and a reduction in sensory disturbances that seem to be different from those produced by simple muscular relaxation. Blood glucose levels of diabetic and normal subjects show that hypnosis brings about homeostatic mechanisms and a sense of well-being. (Weller et al., 1961).

Maiolo, Porro, and Grannone (1969) found that the hypnotic state did not differ from the normal in cerebral haemodynamics and metabolism. However, in the hypnotic state the standard deviations were significantly lower than in waking. Homeostatic factors appear to be more evident for the hypnotic group.

Black and Friedman (1968) found that hypnotic anesthesia produced a significant effect on the pituitary-adrenal access to pain. Black and Wigan (1961) found increased heart rate as a conditioned response could be abolished in hypnotic deafness. To Black and Walter (1965), these findings suggested the possible cerebral level where hypnotic blockage takes place, at least with regard to hearing, probably at some point below the frontal cortex, but above heart-regulating centers in the medula, at the level of the hypothalamus.

Horowitz (1968) observes that images that are emotion arousing and highly meaningful tend to lose their sensory quality only after they are translated into lexical terms. Our observation has been that imagery can be desensitized through repeated exposure.

Since the thinking process plays such an influential role in shaping and influencing sensory and emotion responses, it is important to investigate the properties of words as a perceptual medium to find out what kinds of shape and shape-relation they can provide. Hypnotherapy involving the organization of imagery, and its sensory correlates permit much spontaneous reorganization and freeing of the thought process, which frequently cannot be done through associative uncovering approaches.

Our own investigations imply that hypnosis can initiate abreaction through sensory intensification with imagery, at times with little verbalization but noticeable in polygraphic monitoring. Gellhorn and Loofbourrow (1963) suggest that the physiologic process underlying abreaction is an intensive hypothalamic-cortical discharge followed by a period of lessened cortico-hypothalamic-cortical relations. Following this process, there frequently emerges a relaxed state which, upon careful clinical observation and polygraphic evaluation, resembles a state of exhaustion in which the patient shows a loss of muscle tone and is extremely quiet. This quietness produces a degree of relaxation that is frequently so great as to have not only momentary, but persistent therapeutic value for a very considerable length of time. Abreaction has long been used as a therapeutic device, although its role in psychotherapy continues to be controversial.

Case Illustrations

CASE 1.   A forty-one-year-old married man with gastrointestinal complaints and inability to maintain consistent work patterns was unsuccessful in psychotherapy for four years. Intensive antidepressants and tranquilizing drugs had minimal response. He had a history of disturbed sleep for many years and performed poorly sexually. He found it hard, even upon direction, to talk of anything outside of work and tended to ruminate excessively about his own bodily dysfunctions. He was very tense, sitting on the edge of his chair during the initial interview, talking rapidly, and unable to listen even when the responses were brief and to the point. He described himself as a person who "never could relax" and was certain he could "never be hypnotized." He nevertheless accepted the so-called period of hypnotic training as a prelude to hypnotherapy. His initial reactions to hypnotic induction were anxiety, restlessness, sweating, and near panic. His polygraphic record showed irregular breathing. He disrupted the induction process frequently by talking. Nevertheless, within five hours of hypnotic relaxation he was able to stop his excessive talking. Complete relaxation began by the tenth hour. Five minutes after induction, respiration and GSR were stable and dramatically different from his initial patterns.

He learned to induce hypnosis himself and used it for sleeping easily and soundly and for tense times at work. Instead of talking about his symptoms, he was encouraged to describe his imagery during relaxation. After a month, all somatic symptoms had disappeared. The patient became more concerned about his relationships at work and with his wife. He began to view his sexual difficulty as part of the relationship rather than as a reflection of his previous state of tension. Somatic comfort was now an everyday pattern, and he accepted responsibility for maintaining it.

At a year's follow up, he was still using self-hypnosis about twice a day for ten or fifteen minutes. One of these times was usually an hour before retiring, so that a stabilized sleep pattern was being maintained.

CASE 2. A fifty-two-year-old divorced woman was seen because of extreme anxiety in relation to working. A schoolteacher who had not worked for a number of years following her divorce, she felt rejected and unwanted in the school situation. During years of psychoanalytic therapy, she had recognized some of her own projections and their paranoid quality as being related to her own long-standing insecurity. Nevertheless, she felt so overwhelmed by these feelings that she had on several occasions been forced to leave school, feigning physical illness.

In hypnosis, she could, upon direction, visualize herself in the classroom situation, comfortable and at ease. She also spent a number of hours in hypnosis visualizing herself and gradually correcting her image so that it became spontaneously more and more acceptable and more consistent with reality. She was not unattractive and had gracious manners. Bodily tensions were reduced within several hours of hypnotherapy, and the self-hypnosis was first used five or six times a day and, after three months of therapy, once or twice a day. Among the symptoms the patient presented were marked tremors of both the hands and the head. As she learned to alter the imagery herself, the tremors would spontaneously disappear. She learned rapidly how to influence and direct her own image activity so that by the second month of therapy when she felt the tremors beginning—in the cafeteria at school, or in a teachers' conference—she would within that situation be able to visualize herself calm, relaxed, and at ease, and the impending emergence of tremors would cease.

A year's follow up indicated that she was very gratified by her teaching experience, had found a more desirable teaching assignment with increased salary, and was confident with her use of self-hypnosis.

CASE 3.   This thirty-four-year-old married woman was first seen while still a patient in a state hospital, following a suicide attempt. She had been in psychotherapy for two years for a washing compulsion that so preoccupied her daily life that she was unable to assume her responsibilities for the family. In her most recent analytic therapy, she had spent a good deal of time discussing and uncovering apparent sexual origins for the need to be clean and to wash as many as twenty to thirty times a day. She was unable to touch her hair without feeling that she was contaminated, and any contact with other people or even objects would require frequent hand-washing, as well as long periods of showering and bathing.

During the first three months of therapy, hypnosis was employed primarily to produce complete relaxation, eliminate the need for barbiturates and tranquilizers, and as self-hypnosis for insomnia and reinforcement of the relaxation.

Hypnotic sessions would vary from one- to three-hour periods, during which respiration and muscle tones showed complete relaxation. The patient could remain completely immobile for the entire session. During this period, with increasing vividness, she visualized herself in contact with objects, with people, and with herself. While describing that these contacts made her feel dirty, there was little evidence of bodily tension, and she was able to tolerate the awareness of dirtiness without agitation.

By the fourth month, the patient was no longer taking more than one shower a day, and this never exceeded twenty minutes. She could touch all parts of her body, including her hair, and was able to touch other people as well as to travel in the subways and buses without a feeling of undue contamination. She began to socialize again and, for the first time in four years, to have sexual relations. Her depression vanished, and she began to think seriously about working and resuming responsibility for her family. She enjoyed visiting with her children and spent long periods of time with them.

Self-hypnotic sessions were used by this patient relatively infrequently compared to most of the others in this study.

CASE 4.   A twenty-one-year-old married woman was referred for hypnotherapy by her then fifth therapist. Three months earlier, she had slashed her wrists in an attempt to get herself admitted to the hospital.

The patient had married at the age of seventeen and shortly after had undergone a therapeutic abortion. She had wanted the child and was extremely angry about having it aborted. During the course of marriage, she had tried on a number of occasions to have a child and had a history of three miscarriages, all coinciding with severe emotional disturbance.

The state hospital diagnosis was of a catatonic schizophrenic. However, with hypnosis as a projective and explorative technique, the diagnostic impression was of an hysterical personality with an underlying schizophrenic process. The internist who had treated her since she was fourteen years of age detailed a long history of somatic complaints, some bizarre in nature, most with a tendency toward conversion reactions.

The patient responded exceptionally well to hypnosis, but the use of self-hypnosis was delayed for a considerable period of time in view of her history. Following the first two hour hypnotherapy session, she described improvement in her physical functioning which she said she had never experienced before. A long-standing problem of constipation suddenly vanished, headaches no longer appeared, and the patient described her body as now being fully connected.

Imagery during hypnosis was always vivid and at first, when undirected, tended to assume fantasylike projections not dissimilar to the type of ideational process found in her Rorschach protocols. Directed imagery, on the other hand, tended to be followed rather well and produced effective responses in terms of complete relaxation, the ability to visualize the self in constructive behavior, and, during periods of relaxation, to talk calmly and easily about serious issues between herself and her parents.

After six hypnotic sessions averaging two hours each, the patient felt ease from bodily tensions, was no longer preoccupied with somatic factors, and had reported no periods of agitation. She was not withdrawing into bed, and masturbatory behavior had ceased. In fact, she was able to

discuss fantasies associated with the use of the electric vi-
brator.

Her relationship with her husband improved, and by
the third month of therapy she was employing self-hypnosis regularly, working, and reporting no evidences of agitated, depressed, or hysterical behavior.

After another three months, the patient became pregnant, which at first produced severe anxiety because of the
earlier miscarriages. Self-hypnosis was further developed
for controlling anxiety and somatic distress produced by
the pregnancy. Eventually she had an uncomplicated deliv-
ery. In addition to assuming responsibility for her family,
the patient has taken part-time college courses.

POLYGRAPH RECORDS

The following polygraphic records are representative
illustrations of the nature of hypnotically induced emotions
and the abreactive effects of emotional flooding in sensory
hypnoanalysis,

Figure 6–1 is a typical waking record of an experimen-

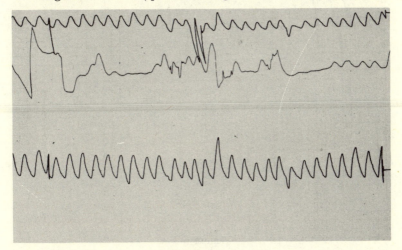

Figure 6-1

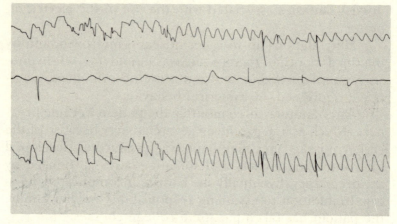

Figure 6-2

tal subject's respiratory (thoracic and abdominal) and GSR patterns on the polygraph.

Figure 6–2 depicts the same subject after ten minutes of hypnosis and "relaxation." At this point in hypnosis

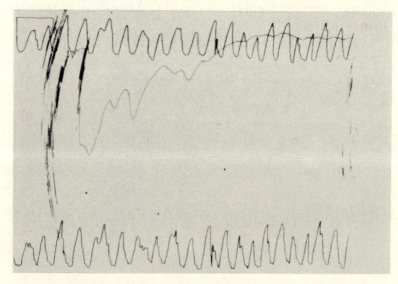

Figure 6-3

there are usually either no significant changes in respiration or—and more likely—there is evidence of increased anxiety at the level as a result of the hypnotic intervention. GSR recordings are usually more stable, however.

Figure 6–3 is the polygraphic record of induced emotion following ten minutes of relaxation. The emotion is produced through the use of hypnotic imagery involving known disturbing elements for the subject. This pattern tends to persist during the monitoring of the imagery and invariably results in an abreactive experience. In this instance, the imagery and abreaction persisted for ten minutes.

Figure 6–4 is the subject's polygraphic recording one hour after the beginning of the experiment, which included a ten-minute waking sequence, a ten-minute period of hypnotic "relaxation," and a ten-minute period of induced emotional disturbance and abreaction. The respiratory and GSR levels obtained in Figure 6–4 begin to assume the pattern recorded at the one-hour level within five minutes of termination of the induced disturbing imagery and the abreactions.

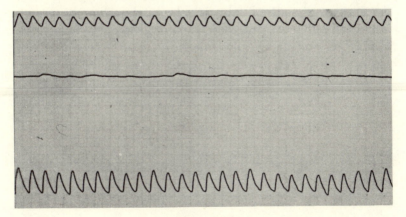

Figure 6-4

SUMMARY

It is clear that not all emotional expression involves the same psychophysiological mechanisms, and those that occur within the framework of the hypnotic transference and the hypnotic state may constitute rather significant differences from those emotions that occur under naturally occuring life involvements and life experiences. This contrast and discrepency is of importance in viewing the nature of emotionally induced behavior, and particularly those therapeutic approaches that may be most valuable in dealing with them.

In sum, it would appear that acute emotional stress induced through hypnosis fails very often to produce those physiological correlates that are typical of naturally occurring emotional stress. The use of encouragement and direction by hypnosis tends to invite abreactive or abreactive-like responses. In addition, the hypnotic transference and its alteration in ego functioning would appear to channel the discharge of emotions in a manner that results in homeostatic adaptation on the part of the patient.

Apart from these considerations, there is much evidence to support the hypothesis that the hypnotic state itself, as well as the hypnotic relationship, has therapeutic value and that its protracted use, particularly in neurotic disorders and psychophysiological disturbances involving autonomic-affective syndromes, may have potentially greater value than has been previously considered.

PART II

Working directly with the patient's body is considered by many practitioners to be the backbone of emotional flooding. Often, bodily manipulation is the only technique used to release intense emotion, with little or no effort aimed at eliciting associative material or "working-through."

Other schools of thought maintain that a variety of techniques —physical and verbal—are necessary in order to stimulate affect, perhaps produce insight, and solidify a patient's gains. Inherent in the emphasis upon the physical is the allied component of action: for example, encounter-type techniques, art methods—in short, activity that encourages the motoric expression of emotion.

Part 2 deals with a wide variety of these methods, from the pioneering and purely physical work of Ida P. Rolf's structural integration to the almost dazzling array of combined techniques used by therapists whose philosophy of treatment is rooted in the ancient maxim that the truth is what works.

chapter 7

STRUCTURAL INTEGRATION: COUNTERPART OF PSYCHOLOGICAL INTEGRATION

Ida P. Rolf, Ph.D.

Most humans think of themselves as a duality—body and soul, body and personality. That is, their self-image calls for "my body" and "me." Their problems, they may feel, are relegated to one or the other of these departments. Consequently, we have two overall divisions of medicine, corresponding roughly to therapy for the body and therapy for the mind. In both, therapists are unhappy. They look at their results and are not satisfied.

Recently more sophisticated thought patterns have nurtured a monistic concept. These premises are demonstrably successful in simultaneously modifying both physical and psychological personality. Through their union both body and ego—that which we refer to as "I"—reach a higher level of mutual peace and mutual acceptance. Among these newer techniques is Structural Integration.

The tendency is to see Structural Integration as a physical, not a psychological, technique. But Structural Integration points up the monistic premise that a human being may be seen as an energy field within the environment of a much greater energy field—the field of the earth's gravity —and this fosters an understanding of human well-being which earlier, more divisive concepts do not permit.

This newer concept demands a realization that relationships rather than isolated factors are the determinants of well-being. It demands the recognition of the physical environment—the field of gravity—as an outstandingly important factor in human well-being. It leads to a new realization; since a two-factored physical system (earth-man) determines human well-being, and since one factor (earth's gravity) is unchangeable, vital change can be effected only through the other factor, man—man as a physical system. We are dealing here with real, not symbolic factors. Our modus operandi is the physical, not the psychological system. But on the basis of our results, we see this physical intervention as a very rapid approach by which to modify the more superficial aspects of the psychological personality.

Physical man—a mechanical system—must be understood and changed in order to let the dual system interact at its best. Thus it is the mechanics of the physical man that must be considered. Approached from this direction, "man" becomes a different entity. To be reinforced by the field of gravity, the physical man must constitute a substantially vertical line through which the gravitational lines of force may flow. In so doing, gravity reinforces and supports the force field of the man.

In this light, bodies are seen as aggregates of segments. As we use the term here, segments are massive body units—head, thorax, pelvis, legs. Aligned so that the center of gravity of each segment is virtually above or below that of its neighbor, these segments unify; they become integrated. Such an alignment gives rise to order within the system—maximum energy organization; minimum randomness; minimum entropic tendency to disorganization, to breakdown, to deterioration. Such an alignment creates a unity between the field of the individual and the field of the earth; it allows the gravitational field to reinforce the energy field of the individual. Under these conditions, the old concept of gravity as the unremitting enemy, the unceasing instigator of physical breakdown, is no longer valid. Gravity becomes a friend.

The inevitable question at this point is: Is it possible to create such a system? Even though the body be segmented, can the segments be drastically realigned? The results of Structural Integration suggest that this ideal physical system, this substantially vertical alignment, can be approached. It is both possible and practical, given certain conditions. In real life, as well as in theory, these controlling conditions can be met.

The body, as we have postulated, is not a single unit; it is an aggregate of segments which attain unity only as the components are stacked vertically one above the other in the three-space of the earth's envelope. In all human bodies, whether vertically ordered or random, weight masses are maintained in their position by the myofascia, that system which has developed from the embryonic mesoderm. When the body is random or aberrated it is the fascia that suffers the most immediate stress. It is the fascia of a body that determines and maintains physical structure. The myofascia may properly be called the organ of structure.

Like all material, fascia may be examined in terms of physical qualities and chemical properties. To effect body change, its physical capacity of resilience is its outstanding quality. Under stress, physical or emotional, fascia shortens. Here the significant fact is that it does not shorten uniformly; certain fascial elements shorten more drastically. Inasmuch as fascial planes throughout the body are connected, such shortening is not limited to a local area but spreads far afield. In addition, "shortening" can happen only by fascial thickening, and in this way we have the beginning of interference with free movement, the beginning of aberrative function.

If the stress be continued, possibly as the result of traumatic accident or illness (pathological change) invading one or more local areas or organs, the fascia under stress may change chemically. Or it may secrete an exudate in an effort at self-lubrication or in response to some invading element, viral or bacterial. As the situation progresses, the exudate, instead of disappearing completely, seems to dry out, leaving a residual "glue" that fastens adjacent fascial planes together. These planes have been individually shortened by the disease process; the result is a muscular patch no longer able to stretch sufficiently to effect the pumping action that is the physiological function of muscles and myofascia. In consequence, the chemistry of the area further deteriorates. Exchange of metabolites becomes inadequate, oxygen supply is interfered with, and the nutritional level is lowered. Eventually this area, originally characterized by muscular resilience and movement, becomes immobile; the "muscle" becomes "gristle," and local movement of fascial planes on neighboring fascial planes is no longer possible. This deterioration may be limited to a space the size of a pea or walnut, or it may involve a much larger area, such as the entire muscular pad covering the sacrum, the health of which is so necessary to pelvic well-being. The end result is a patch of markedly lowered energy.

Unfortunately, deterioration of a fascial area cannot be limited to that area, nor can the lowered level of energy be localized. Just as a snag in a knitted jacket may well pull the entire fabric askew, so this snag in the fascial fabric may pull the entire myofascial structure out of alignment. And just as the repair of a snag in the knitting will of necessity call for reorganizing the wool at points of strain far from the original snag so balancing myofascial stress in the body requires work in areas far from the originating trauma. Organically the fascia is one interconnecting set of planes, and damage to any point travels as so-called compensations throughout the body. Reorganization must start with these compensations, not with the point of origin. Since the body is vital and alive, the lessened strain as these compensations are lightened permits the beginning of a spontaneous rehabilitating process. The end point of this process, if it is to be permanently effective, is the establishment of vertical alignment between neighboring segments. In turn, vertical alignment means that a body can avail itself of a gravitational reinforcement that further raises the energy level of this man-earth system.

The practice of Structural Integration calls for the addition of energy by manual pressure from a practitioner. Its targets are areas of fascial stress in the body of the individual to be changed. To create an ordered body, energy must be added in ordered, not random, progression. This ordered pattern constitutes the science and art of the method. The body can be organized or reorganized by adding energy. Pressure appropriately directed by the practitioner is one way of adding energy. Another physiological change is equally important in increasing the free body energy. Release of fascial planes that have become glued together also augments available energy. When a fascial plane is free to slide over its neighbor, much less energy is required on the part of the body to effect a given movement. In either case, the total effect seems to be a greater energy reservoir available for use. The basic condition which makes these changes possible is that each large vertical segment shall fit over the one below.

Rehabilitation of the body as a whole proceeds from joint to joint and requires freeing and reorganizing joints. In this connection, the word "joint" applies less to bony interfaces than to the adjacent soft tissue—ligaments and tendons. Their tone and precise direction determines the fashion in which the bony surfaces of the joints can perform. Of particular importance is the ankle, since it is through organization here that body weight balances with reference to the earth's horizontal.

Freeing the body must be done in ordered progression, from segment to segment, joint to joint. Thus changes at the knee joint presupposes prior liberation of the ankle. Since the hip joint involves the proximal end of the femur, of necessity change in the hip requires free mobility at the distal end of the femur, in the knee.

Of the various body segments, the pelvis is primary in importance. Horizontal planes in the pelvis permit adequate performance by basic contributors to physical well-being. The autonomic nervous system and its plexi, as well as the more obvious reproductive and eliminative systems are related and balanced within the pelvic floor. If in a standing figure the line connecting the coccyx with the pubic ramus is horizontal, the floor of the pelvis will be horizontal. The existence of this horizontal also makes sagittal balance possible, and the two anterior superior spines will be equidistant from the vertical line rising through the center of the pubes.

Many therapeutic systems have been built on the idea that a balanced spine (including balance between individual vertebrae as well as larger units—lumbar, dorsal, cervical, et cetera) is necessary for well-being. Up to this point in time, however, no general agreement has been reached as to what constitutes a balanced spine. Our contribution to this controversy is simple. We claim that a spine can be truly balanced only as it is based on a balanced—a horizontal—pelvis. If a body is to utilize the gravitational field to enhance its own energy, the pelvis in its home position must be in equipoise. In addition to being horizontal, it must be capable of free rotational adjustment around the head of the femur. Only under these conditions can the bony basin readjust and create the balance necessary to good functional support. Since the foot must necessarily conform to the earth, a pelvis can be horizontal only if there is free spontaneous adjustment possible at hip, knee, and ankle. In turn, this implies that legs are straight. In walking, the knees of such legs trace a line straight forward and straight back. It is the basic hinge action at the ankle that permits this straight-line movement. The knee will adjust if the ankle permits change. Knee and ankle have freedom of motion only if placement in space of the ligaments and tendons that determine joint function is appropriate.

The question at this point is obvious. How can appropriate organization of these joints be induced? First of all, the practitioner must have a clear picture of where individual muscles should lie and to what extent they must be changed to permit this kind of movement. This he determines by inspection of external body contour. Visual assay can be validated by palpation. No soft tissue area should impress his hands as tough, immobile, or wooden. Normal areas are resilient; the movement of individual muscle, ligament, and tendon can be felt through the entire depth of the tissue. If such movement is not apparent in the body contour, myofascial elements are either "glued" or have deteriorated. Such tissue must be worked with—that is, energy must be added—until it is free.

Addition of energy at this level is far from superficial massage. In Structural Integration, the practitioner recognizes which muscles are displaced from the pattern; he then manually brings this soft tissue toward the normal position and demands that the related joint or part perform its appropriate physiological movement while the tendon or muscle is being held as near to its normal position as possible. Suddenly the muscle moves in a more appropriate pattern. The patient often feels release far afield from the specific area manipulated.

This bonus, by which liberating one specific area frees

and reorganizes very distant structures, is possible because of the nature of fascia. For fascia is ubiquitous. Every muscle and every organ, through its enwrapping fascia, is structurally connected with every other muscle and organ of the body. It is not possible that any one local area of fascia be shortened, thickened, or congested, either temporarily or permanently, without giving rise to tensions throughout the body. Some of these inevitably will be more direct, more immediate, more specific than others. These probably constitute the reflex points. But all need release, for tensions betray malfunction. Hypertensions must give way to normal tone in order that maximum efficiency may be restored to a body.

When pelvis and legs are appropriately and freely related, the task of aligning a body is more than well begun. A horizontal pelvis makes a free, adjustable base for the spine. In turn, this offers stable, vertically aligned support for the cranium, container of the great nervous plexus, the brain. Skillful organization of upper body structures is still necessary to create the vertical man. But without appropriate support from the pelvis, the task is impossible.

The same basic principles can be applied throughout the body; fascial restrictions can be lessened. This nurtures appropriate movement and makes effective use of the freed structure possible. Such movement permits the body to use its environmental gravity field to enhance its own energy. The body pattern that permits this type of movement is characteristic in form. The more closely an individual conforms to it, the more efficiently he can function. Efficient structure is synonymous with efficient joints. In liberating structure by way of body joints, movement is freed. In turn, joint competence, including vertebral joints, seems to underlie and determine visceral function. A great sense of general well-being, far more profound than the greater movement warrants, accompanies improved joint performance.

At any level, behavior is function. Behavior has been called psychology, and classically it has been attributed to nervous and/or glandular function. But behavior is more than the expression of a single body system. It is also an expression of relationship, of physical relationship, the relationship of individual physical parts to each other and of these parts to the whole man. It is the relationship of a physical—a structured—man, in himself an energy unit, to his physical energy environment—gravity. A sense of well-being, of peace and of creative capacity, is the individual's awareness of integrated physiological function.

Structural Integration has a proper place as basic among the psychotherapeutic techniques. For psychological hang-ups are recorded and perpetuated in the physical body in flesh and in bones. As long as such hang-ups persist in physical bodies, psychological release is interfered with. Conversely, the release of the body distortion, while not necessarily obviating the later skilled services of a psychotherapist, makes his work easier, quicker, and more effective. The findings of Structural Integration emphasize that the more quickly we can recognize the unity of body and mind, the more effective will be our intervention from either direction.

chapter 8

EMOTIONAL FLOODING AND BIOENERGETIC ANALYSIS

John M. Bellis, M.D.

Emotional flooding and emotional drought are the Scylla and Charybdis of human development. One may give rise to neurosis or character disorder and the other to psychosis. Both interfere characteristically with physical as well as psychological development, depending upon the intensity and the duration of stress and the ego-development of the individual victim. Failure of the victim in attaining an adequate defense against extremes of environmental stimulation may result in ego disintegration, physical breakdown, or death. The schizoid survivor of infantile drought or deprivation may be more than usually susceptible to emotional flooding, while the neurotic adapter to emotional flooding may be more liable to breakdown under conditions of emotional deprivation.

What are we talking about? We are talking about external stimulation, or lack of it, beyond the adaptive (ego) capacity of the individual to respond integratively, that is, as a whole person.

What do the victims of emotional flooding and emotional drought have in common? They both are flooded by internal feelings, instinctual urges, and reflex responses, leading in either case to rage, panic, terror, or despair. It is this internal flooding that is the subject of this chapter.

Both emotional flooding and emotional drought have been widely used in therapy; usually, however, in homeopathic doses. Psychoanalysis, for example, has made perhaps the most famous and widest use of what I have called here emotional drought in the deprivation of the patient of physical contact, visual contact, and expected responses. Modifications of techniques in psychoanalysis are recognized as mandatory in certain character structures and at certain times in treatment.

Behavioral therapy appears to utilize both emotional drought and emotional flooding. Wolpe's carefully modulated schedule of rewards and punishments and re-enactments of traumatic experience as well as the magnificently intuitive and poetic techniques of Thomas Stampfl appear to be cases in point.

Every clinician must understand and calibrate his own instruments and carefully evaluate his patient's capacity to withstand stress, adapting the former to the latter. No technique is therapeutic in itself. No response to a therapeutic intervention is therapeutic in itself either, unless it occurs in a setting of expectance and understanding and can be integrated into the patient's view of himself and the world.

Even the long sought after abreaction—and its modern equivalent, the primal—can be antitherapeutic, humiliating, and devastating to the remaining resources of the individual unless it occurs at the right time, in the right setting, and can be integrated by the patient.

The concept of emotional flooding, in the genesis of emotional illness as well as in the treatment of it, are therefore not original or indigenous to bioenergetic analysis. I hope it will be seen, however, that the concept rather easily finds a home there. In order to demonstrate this, however, it will be necessary to describe in some detail two basic concepts in bioenergetic analysis—character armoring and grounding. Character armor will be described first.

CHARACTER ARMOR—THE LAYERS OF THE ONION

Bioenergetic analysis is a psychoanalytically derived theory of character structure and technique of character analysis based upon the work of Wilhelm Reich and Alexander Lowen. I quote from Dr. Lowen:

> Experiences must be accompanied by insight if they are to have a positive effect upon the personality. The most difficult thing for therapists to learn is character analysis. While it is relatively easy to give a person an experience or even open up a feeling, it is much more difficult to help that person integrate the experience on a characterological level.
>
> Since the character is the sum total of all tension patterns, it is expressed in the form and motility of the body. Reading the body characterologically is the sign of a good bioenergetic therapist. Working with the body characterologically is what distinguishes bioenergetic analysis from other body approaches which do not have the character analytic basis. [Lowen 1971]

Wilhelm Reich's contribution to our understanding of character structure lay in his emphasis on the muscular basis of character armor and on his insistence upon finding a physical basis for the libido theory in the energy economy of the body. He called this energy orgone energy, deriving it from the term organismic. Since we are now once again searching beyond ego psychology to such energetic and body concepts as emotional flooding, it is not surprising that his views are once again being widely reviewed.

Masking

The first and best known function of character armoring is that of masking. This is also widely known as "facework" and involves not only the psychological attitudes necessary to maintain social position and role but also more than considerable energy. In doing so, it utilizes the muscles of the face working in conjunction with the eyes, jaw, and neck, and indirectly the whole body which supports the mask. The chief ego function of this layer of muscular armoring is to assist the individual in maintaining a certain role in his family and social structure by hiding; or, perhaps more accurately, indicating that he wishes to hide certain feelings that he deems inappropriate to his role at that time. His family and social peers pick up these cues and assist him in supporting his role or the "face" that he indicates he wishes to maintain on that occasion.

While this function of armoring is an extremely important one, especially in analyzing the psychological relationship of the individual to society, it is also important to understand it in terms of its function in blocking energy. The facial muscles are the most superficial muscles; they are derived from the cutaneous layer, which is also closest to awareness. It is also the layer to which most of us respond in judging at what distance and emotional intensity we can relate to the individual. Behind the individual's mask we can always see what he really feels in his eyes, and we often hear it in his voice, if this is not too choked or blocked. From his mask, we pick up the cues as to what it is appropriate to respond. Unless we enjoy a particularly intimate or authoritative relationship with him, however, we rarely, if ever, go behind the mask directly.

The mask thus blocks or modulates the energy input from the social environment. At the same time the mask also blocks the outpouring of both conscious and preconscious affect. This energetic phenomenon can be demonstrated in two ways: first, by pressure over certain parts of the face, for example, by taking away a person's smile, by pressure over the risorious muscle; second, by asking the patient to make a face as children do—if this face is also connected with an appropriate voice, as in growling like a lion, the individual may experience a sudden coming alive of the energy in him that is often unavailable behind his conventional mask. Children, of course, make wide use of this latter mechanism to energize much of their play.

The Long Skeletal Muscles

A second layer of muscular character armor is that of the long skeletal muscles of the body, both the extensors and the flexors. This layer, the most massive layer of muscles of the body, protects the individual from being overwhelmed, either by his instinctual impulses or by stimulation from the outside world, by holding within it a potential for movement. It plays an important role in our homeostasis by binding such energy until it is appropriate to discharge it in activity in motion. These long skeletal muscles, by tensing and binding energy, or by discharging it, either in random or purposive movement, protect the individual from internal flooding. When this system is overwhelmed and internal flooding occurs, it may be manifest in such acute psychophysiological reactions of the autonomic nervous system as diarrhea, vomiting, and urinary incontinence, and also in acute central nervous system responses that partially or completely cloud our consciousness, resulting in dizziness, fainting, "blowing our tops," or inappropriate hysterical behavior. The binding of energy in our muscles helps us control our inner environment and at the same time keep our heads, the better to control or respond adaptively to the outer world.

The first sign, usually, that these muscles are reaching

their adaptive homeostatic capacity is their trembling, as from excitement, fatigue, and stretching. Stretching appears to diminish the ability of the muscle to hold energy. Another sign that muscles are overloaded in their adaptive function is pain. This usually occurs when the muscle is knotted under prolonged stress; gritting one's teeth results in pain not only of the gums but more directly in the masseter muscles themselves and in the temporalis muscles.

Muscles of the Joints and Sphincters

A third layer of muscular armoring, on an even deeper level, although much less massive, helps to prevent emotional flooding and overwhelming response to emotional deprivation through a somewhat different mechanism. Through the use of partly voluntary, and partly involuntary muscles at the strictures and sphincters of the body, the flow within the organism and the outflow of energies into the environment is controlled, much as the damage-control bulwarks of a ship assist in maintaining stability. This type of armoring is segmental and involves as yet poorly understood responses in the ocular segment, in the jaw, throat, chest, shoulder girdle, diaphragm, abdomen, and pelvis.

It is common to divide these segmental armoring layers into seven segments, although many subdivisions can be discerned in some individuals.

Segmental armoring has a capacity somewhat similar to that of an annelid worm. It takes up stress in one segment when it is released in another. For example, if the diaphragmatic segment—that is to say, the breathing of the individual—is loosened and freed, his throat—his voice—may become choked, or his jaw may clench as though holding against the energy released by the improved breathing. Similar mechanisms may occur when the energy is loosened in the pelvis at a time or in circumstances unacceptable to the ego. This is common, for example, when someone is blocking the impulse to cry. He customarily does so by reducing his breathing to a minimum, gritting his teeth, and tightening in the throat, resulting in a "lump" in the throat. If one or another segment is loosened, the others will tighten up or the individual will start to cry (to flow).

The Diaphragm and the Semivoluntary Muscles of Digestion, Respiration, and the Voice

This layer of muscular armoring is often included in the third layer mentioned above, but there is, I think, a sufficiently good reason to differentiate it, at least for didactic purposes. The diaphragm itself, which is derived embryologically via the phrenic nerve from the neck and throat segments, serves the obviously homeostatic function of the control of energy intake; with the other semivoluntary muscles of respiration, it can increase the amount of oxygen intake into the system in states of readiness and excitement. It may also sharply curtail the energy available in the system in states of anxiety through the immobilization of the muscles of respiration in the head, neck, and chest. These same muscles, or combination of muscles, may also block any outcry that might betray us in times of stress. When this stress is chronic and the response of the individual organism is a chronic curtailment of energy intake and emotional expression, it results in a deadening of the body and alienation from the body. This deadening or alienation process is the hallmark of our society, but it is most clearly seen in a chronic schizophrenic. It may also be seen in many other conditions.

The hyperventilation syndrome, for example, is often thought to be, as its name implies, a symptom of overcharging or of anxiety. Actually it occurs in individuals who chronically underventilate and who begin to panic when they experience a sudden surcharge of feeling. This precipitates the rather well-known vicious cycle of hyperventilation.

The voice, on a social level, is as important as breathing on a biological level. In practice the two are related. It is well known that crying and other vocal sounds enhance breathing. Every release phenomena is accompanied by sound, unless the release itself is partially choked, along with the voice. A full and open voice resonates from within the entire body, as in singing. The singing voice as well as the laughing voice of man are the two ego functions closest to the heart, metaphorically as well as in actuality. Ego maturity may be said to have been achieved when an individual has a voice in his community. We are all familiar as clinicians with how much can be gained by listening to the quality of the voice, sometimes much more than one can gain by the words themselves.

It is this deepest layer of armoring that modulates the most essential functions of life including our breathing, our voice, and our digestion, and perhaps gives our every act its special tone.

GROUNDING

The main contribution of Alexander Lowen to the character analytic work of Wilhelm Reich, I believe, is in his concepts of grounding. Lowen's concept of grounding is perhaps closest to the Freudian notion of the reality principle and to the ability of the ego to ground, contain, and integrate feelings aroused by him both by his psychosexual development and by his environment. Character traits and character armoring as discussed in the foregoing parts of this chapter are derived and understood mostly in terms of the pleasure principle and the psychosexual development of the individual. The functions of grounding, containment, and integration, on the other hand, are much more relevant to the development of the ego and to its most basic functions: (1) its motor function—standing, rising, walking, and handling the world; (2) its perceptual functions, including the integration of what is heard and seen with its motor functions and advancing to conceptualization, understanding, and wisdom; and (3) its vocal functions—to the point where each person attains his own voice and harmonizes his heart with his ego functions.

Grounding and Motor Function

The function of grounding with respect to the ego motor function relate most directly to the relationship of the individual to the field of gravity. In bioenergetic analysis we find it routinely born out, for example, in our clinical evaluation of people that those who do not have their feet on the ground—who have very poor feeling and motor connection with the ground, literally, in their feet and legs —are not well grounded on a psychological level either. In fact, it is striking how frequently the metaphors of common speech have a very relevant, clinically confirmable, foundation. A person who, psychologically speaking, has very little backbone is usually found clinically and literally to have a very poor sense of where his backbone is. He is often collapsed, and his ability to move as well as to sustain postural balance is sharply curtailed. Just as in psychoanalytic theory, we find that primitive attempts to survive on the part of the infant child that necessitate suppression of the pleasure principle result in difficulties in the motor functions of the individual. For example, patients with excessively intrusive mothers at the anal stage will demonstrate defects of motor function stemming from excessive sphincter control and tightening of the laveter ani muscles, the gluteals. At the same time he will generally have lost the sense of where his heels are, having abandoned kicking for withholding. Such a person, in the extreme, may walk like a duck.

Perceptual Functions and the Functions of Grounding

The chief segments through which we ground ourselves in social reality are our visual and auditory segments. When these segments have been blocked by terror in early phases of life, perception—including such basic functions as reading—is often interfered with. The myopic individual permits just enough feeling to come through his eyes so that he can handle the emotional charge involved and process it through his mental computer. Myopes are generally known to be intellectuals and in general to be somewhat insensitive emotionally, at least to stimuli coming through the ocular segment. They are most responsive, in other words, emotionally to things at close contact and have deadened their emotional responses to distant threats. It is obvious, of course, that such functions on a bodily level may be compensated by a hyperactive mind and perhaps hyperaggressiveness on an intellectual level. People suffering from hyperopia, by contrast, often miss what is under their nose and tend to keep people at a distance where they can be responded to emotionally with greater clarity. A person cannot be said to be fully grounded in his reality function until his eyes are opened, not only in an optical sense but on a feeling level. Severe distortions of both the ocular and aural functions on an emotional level often result in distortions in hearing and vision on a more mechanical level.

Grounding and the Vocal Functions of the Ego

At the point where a person attains his own voice and harmonizes his heart with his ego function—his feelings with the reality principle—he may be said to have achieved maturity. It is interesting to note the derivation of the word person from persona; through one's voice or sound one knows a person. When one has achieved a voice, one has achieved maturity. While complete maturity may depend upon the ability of the individual to possess all of his introjected family—all his irrational feelings and attitudes, the myths and illusions that have surrounded his birth and development— he has not become a person until he has found the confidence to speak for himself.

Grounding Techniques

Grounding is attained in bioenergetic analysis through assisting the person to get in touch with himself, the language of his body, the language of his parts, the language of his introjects, however one wishes to conceptualize this. One of the techniques introduced by Lowen which has much potential for exploring this diversity of inner experience is that of pitting the person against the field of gravity in such a way that he is encouraged to bring out his negative attitudes against giving in or collapsing. After having done so, he is enabled thereby to give in to the inevitable, to the reality of life. Utilizing the field of gravity in place of other social stresses gives the therapist the advantage of confronting the patient with reality on a here-and-now basis in the office. When an individual is able to give in to the inevitable tug of gravity and thus to at least one reality of life—the reality of gravity—he is usually enabled thereby to attempt this in other circumstances in life. As we all know, clinically, a person who is terrified of collapse has difficulty in falling asleep as well as falling in love and giving in and letting go in other ways. This will interfere with his pleasure functions and ultimately result in a collapse of part of the body in physical disease, or in emotional symptoms that often herald such a collapse, and constrict the behavior of the individual.

It is interesting to ask what it is in each individual's ego structure which opposes reality to the extent that a person is unrealistic—we think of him as neurotic or even psychotic. Those ego structures that oppose reality or deny it are usually found to be based upon negative attitudes toward our parents or those who nurture us; from the point of view of reality those negative attitudes incorporate into themselves the child's view of reality at the time that he was subjected to stress. Our neuroses incorporate illusions based upon the narcissistic view of the world, of the infant or child at the time that his neurotic defenses were necessitated.

It is always necessary, when working physically on the grounding of an individual, to uncover these attitudes and illusions. It is in this process, popularly known as head-shrinking, that an individual's sense and acceptance of his body grow on a realistic level, and his illusions diminish.

Other techniques of bioenergetic analysis may be categorized into expressive techniques where the individual is asked to express in his motor and vocal functions certain emotions through kicking and hitting and so on. These techniques are directed not only to the discharge of affect but to an increase in the ability of the individual to focus his energies and thus to ground himself in reality. Other techniques that are designed to improve breathing and the energy level of the individual are also related to grounding in the sense that they require for the proper ego development the ability to handle such energies and to utilize them appropriately. This involves sometimes not only expression but containment.

EMOTIONAL FLOODING IN THERAPY

It cannot be emphasized too much, especially in this day and age when techniques of emotional flooding and emotional deprivation are being used with such great enthusiasm, that a breakthrough or an achievement of release solves very little in an individual's search for himself; that is to say, in his search for self-possession.

It is possible, of course, sometimes ridiculously easy to release symptoms as a result of an emotional release, a primal, or a breakthrough. It is also generally known that most people feel better after a good cry or after getting something off their chest, or even after vomiting. This is not to say, however, that their ego is any stronger, that they are better grounded in reality in their ability to move, to perceive, to speak for themselves, to possess themselves. It is not to say that they will be any more creative, except possibly for a short period following the release when they have much more available energy. It is true, however, that the achievement of emotional release can be dramatic and can be convincing and can be even contagious. It may lend an aura of truth to anything that is believed or taught by the practitioner. It may become the basis of many religious conversions and what is commonly called "healing." Unfortunately, it may also work to build up a sense of unreality in the practitioner. This type of breakthrough occurs much more readily in groups where more energy is available to overwhelm the defensive structure of the individual.

The work of grounding in reality, the work, that is, of psychotherapy, of shrinking the head, of assisting the individual to contain and to integrate his experience, remains a task of the psychotherapist, of whatever brand or persuasion. An hysteric, as we all know, may have many dramatic breakthroughs, may have many dramatic insights, without any essential change in himself. All of us, as experienced clinicians, I am sure, have been tantalized and have indulged ourselves in "cures" in which we have little faith. Thus, like everything else which is powerful, emotional flooding may have its dangers as well as its benefits.

The particular relevance of bioenergetic analysis to the concept of emotional flooding is in its emphasis on the functions of grounding and reality which it contributes along with the vast outpouring of techniques from all quarters designed to improve communications, closeness, intimacy, expression, opening up, and so forth. We, too, utilized many of these techniques, but our basic "technique" is our understanding of the patient's character and his grounding. Until the individual can accept and deal with reality, essentially the reality of himself, and until he is self-possessed, he is neither mature nor integrated, and his improvement or cure may well be ephemeral.

APPLICATIONS OF BIOENERGETIC ANALYSIS

Any method of treatment must be adapted to the expectations and world view of the patient. Thus, a patient who sees his problem only in psychological terms is not likely to welcome a physical method of treatment. Someone who sees his problems only in terms of the limitations of his life or of his vocational situation is not likely to welcome anything but manipulation of the environment or shrewd advice and support. An elderly patient may wish only symptom relief and have little heart for any basic change in himself. A patient with a compensation neurosis may have reason to dread any successful outcome to his treatment, no matter what technique is used. Young people, in general, have very little sense of the limitations of character but always hope that the next day of life may offer them a respite from their difficulties; and so they are not likely to welcome any method of treatment that involves them deeply in a commitment. Some people see treatment only in terms of chemcial change and will accept only medication.

Apart from the world view of the patient, however, bioenergetic analysis, like any method of treatment, is not so much limited by its techniques as it is by the understanding and the ability of the therapist to open his heart and to feel the struggle of the individual whom he is working with in that individual's terms but with the therapist's feelings. If the therapist himself, in other words, has not felt in himself and come to possess his own incestual feelings, his homosexual feelings, his murderous rage, his fear, his terror, his horror, he is to that extent limited in his ability, no matter what technique or method he uses in dealing with his patients. He will then be able to deal with them only cognitively. While he may be helpful in the advice and assistance that he offers, both the patient and the therapist will know at some level that he cannot take the patient any further than he himself has gone on his road toward self-possession.

chapter 9

THE MOBILIZATION OF AFFECT IN WOMEN THROUGH ART

Margaret Frings Keyes, M.S.W.

Using art material to make images brings into the open feelings and thoughts that have been only vaguely sensed. Figure and ground alternate with increased awareness and closure becomes possible for unfinished issues that push for resolution. This is most apparent in reconnecting to unfinished or blocked feelings of the loss-grieving cycle. Art media facilitate release of intense affect in psychotherapy when they are included in the design of treatment.

Women often come to therapy in a grieving state—death; divorce; loss of a parent, a lover, or a child; loss of role; loss of "face" (self-image); failure to make a scholastic or professional goal; loss of a feeling of self-worth and meaning. All of these set in motion a sequence of reactions that can be looked at as variants of the grieving cycle and treated as such. The sequence is never as uncomplicated as shown in the following diagrams, but the art processes indicate possibilities for deepening the emotional experi-

Figure 9–1
THE LOSS-GRIEVING CYCLE

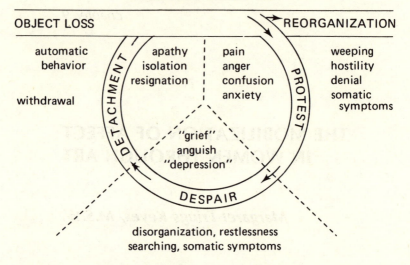

OBJECT LOSS   REORGANIZATION

automatic   apathy   pain   weeping
behavior   isolation   anger   hostility
                 resignation confusion   denial
                             anxiety   somatic
withdrawal   symptoms

DETACHMENT   PROTEST

                "grief"
                anguish
                "depression"

                DESPAIR

disorganization, restlessness
searching, somatic symptoms

Source. The loss-grieving cycle is based on the sequence outlined by John Bowlby, M.D. and developed by William M. Lamers, Jr., M.D.

ence and eliciting appropriate behavioral responses that may have been blocked.

Following loss there are three periods of reaction: protest, despair, and detachment. After detachment a period of reorganization begins. Inside the circle are the emotional aspects as they are experienced within the person, while on the outside of the circle are the behavioral counterparts we observe. During the phase of protest, tears serve as a sign of distress and a signal for help. Hostility is both anger at the object for going away and, in a sense, a warning to it never to go away again; but it is also directed toward the self as self-blame for having caused the rupture. Denial allows belief that what the senses say has happened has not. Memory disturbance functions in the same way. Somatic symptoms, sighing respiration, musclar weakness, disturbed sleep, and diminished appetite, indicate the felt need and dependency. Despair is outwardly manifested in

Figure 9-2
ART PROCESSES RELATED TO PHASES OF LOSS-GRIEVING CYCLE

Phase	Process	Purpose
Protest	Sculpting relationships	To develop feelings toward parent, mate, child.
	Family sculpt	To develop Transactional Analysis (TA) injunctions that the therapist can use to trigger bioenergetic exercises and Altered State of Consciousness (ASC) early family scenes to work through and experience feelings that are blocked.
	Clay smearing	Regression, developing disgust and anger.
	Shadow collage	To connect with projected feelings.
	Painting body work	Contacting and connecting body constriction, areas of deadness, evidence of loss, hurt, images of what was, what was and is wanted, yearnings.
Despair	Painting feelings	To develop images of inner and outer aspects of loss, of felt conflicts, later used in integration painting, polarization, and dialogue painting; to identify tension within or in relation to partner.
	Painting dream images —with psychodrama —with videotape	To enter into the feelings of blackness, emptiness. Deepening the feelings of loss, saying goodbye, ending, finishing.
Detachment	Use of myth—beginnings and rebirth, inclusion of darkness.	To identify the knowledge gained, to recognize and to contain the feelings within images, to connect them to a process of transformation.

Reorganization	Painting dreams, mandalas	To stimulate activity and further the work of integration and growth, mandalas to identify and contain opposite feelings ("both/and" rather than "either/or").
	Collage and dialogue with the luminous shadow	To identify unsuspected growth areas.
	Painting images from ASC fantasies	To further analogous thought of options and possibilities.

disorganization, restlessness, and searching. Inwardly, there is anguish and depression. During the period of detachment, emotional affect tends to flatten into apathy and resignation. Outer behavior is automatic, with a tendency to withdraw from regular patterns and a diminished tolerance of interpersonal relationships. If the loss can be integrated and new relationships formed that are rewarding in themselves, personality reorganization and reintegration can take place.

Even as art processes are effective in the release of feelings in the loss-grieving cycle, so I have found them of great value in assisting clients to release blocked feelings of suppressed anger, guilt, fear, and so on, especially in the context of intensive daily treatment, either individual or group.

Working with an individual, I prefer to start with ten consecutive days in which the client comes each morning and works for as long as something meaningful is occurring —usually one to two and a-half hours. She keeps a daily journal that can be used in any fashion, although I sometimes suggest a specific exercise such as dialogue with a dream figure or between two polarized aspects of herself that she has uncovered. She also paints her primary dream of the previous night. These paintings force choice in selection of symbol and form, emphasis, and use of color. The feeling context is vividly present to be used in Gestalt fashion.

There is no characteristic art method to start treatment. The client always begins with that which makes her most anxious. Sometimes I use a videotaping session near the beginning. I set the camera to take in a full body view, then I leave her alone for fifteen to twenty minutes to make a statement about herself, how she views her situation, what she wants to change or have changed. When I return, we look at this portion together, sometimes replaying a section to which I particularly want to call her attention, then I reset the camera for a close-up face focus and we begin our discussion of what we have seen. She carries this discussion, and I make only minimal comments to facilitate it.

It seems that most of us program our behavior and our communication in terms of how we expect to be perceived. We modify this in terms of interactional clues. The session alone with the camera is difficult. How it was difficult becomes a topic to discuss, as well as the expression of tension in body and voice—what this voice sounds like and seems to be saying apart from the word content. All of this she observes and then comments on how she came across to herself, often spontaneously noting connections to family members in aspects of her style. I may ask her to exaggerate and build up some element of voice or gesture to make the feeling more explicit. Then, as I rewind the tape, I suggest that she make a quick sketch of the image she now has of her body, exaggerating the areas of tension. This discussion is usually exciting, and when the close-up picture and discussion is shown she experiences herself in still another way. The expressive use of eyes and mouth, unguarded and largely unself-conscious—she now sees them, usually for the first time. She also observes added components of her interactive style, her push or hesitancy, her need to explain.

With one client, Addie, her voice clearly did not fit with her body. It sounded to her like her mother's—a woman who was very uncertain of her own value and place with her husband, and who displaced much of her anxiety onto Addie, forcing her to have her teeth straightened and capped and her nose bobbed. As Addie remembered, her conversations with her mother were mostly about food and diets and how fat she was. The mother also gave and withheld gifts. The therapeutic question now became why Addie was still carrying her parent around in her body and what this had to do with her difficulties—notably, her periods of inability to be productive in her profession as a photographer, during which time she would gain huge amounts of weight.

The next session involved deep relaxation exercises and the induction of a light trance state in which Addie regressed to childhood and re-experienced specific incidents with her mother. I suggested that, if she were willing, it might be useful to work with clay at this point in order to get into her feelings about her body; and that if she felt like making noises or flinging the clay, she might do so. As she stripped to her underpants, I laid out a large vinyl dropcloth and twenty-five pounds of moist brown clay in the art room. She worked alone in complete absorption for close to three hours—at first with two figures she called "thick Addie" and "thin Addie." Thick Addie looked like a pregnant mother goddess with pendulous breasts; thin Addie, a starved stick.

She then began to smear the clay in circles, making low rumbling sounds in her throat. Finally anger erupted in words as she pulled at the clay, clenched it, and flung it at the floor screaming, "You slut, filthy bitch, whore. . . ." As her screams rose, tears emerged, and her angry words became more incoherent. Finally she collapsed to the floor into the now considerable mess she had created, sobbing, smearing her body, her face, and her hair. Small whimpering sounds, then: "Mommy, love me, *love me!* Why don't you love me? Why don't you like me the way I am?" I entered at this point and sat beside her. She put her head on my lap, arms around my waist, and cried wordlessly for many minutes while I held her and softly massaged and patted her back. This was the beginning work on her self-hatred and the polarized feelings of anger, hurt, and longing that she still held for her mother, the inner conflict she felt about bearing a baby and thickening her body, the feelings she had about her own engulfing qualities in any close relationship.

Art materials reach different levels of the personality than words alone. I use clay for its sensory tactile qualities and capacity to bring out primitive anal, sexual feelings, feelings of disgust and engulfment, but clients often use it in extremely personal symbolic ways. In one instance I brought in a married couple for a completely nonverbal session. Both were professionals, the wife a clinical psychologist, her husband a physicist. She tended to avoid her feelings by speculating on the reasons for his behavior. He largely retreated into inarticulate anger. I put a partition between them and had them each work with clay to depict what their relationship felt like, then the relationship to the most problematic parent for each, and, finally, to their child. It was not until this session, looking at her husband's sculpt of a wall separating her from him and their son that the wife recognized how deeply identified her husband was with their mentally defective son, who had been put into foster care shortly after infancy when the mother felt his care to be too burdensome for her own career. She realized that her husband felt that he, too, was expendable to her driving ambition. As they talked, she could begin to share the extent to which ambition was a cover for her own feelings of vulnerability rooted in a reaction to the "helplessness" of her mother.

Most clients identify the family sculpt as the most useful art experience in therapy, even though it starts out as a transactional analysis head trip. I ask my client to go back to a time in childhood, somewhere between two and eight years old, to think about who was present in the family at that point and how they related. He or she now lists two or three adjectives or descriptive phrases for each person and makes a clay sculpt of the adjectives, including those applied to himself. When the figures are finished, he arranges them to show their relationship; who was close to him and who was far away. Perhaps someone was "on top" of someone else in the family. He now writes a message from each family member to himself about his worth or how to behave, and finally his answer to each message.

Anna depicted her family, then realized that she had received paternal messages that life was a struggle. She must work hard but, since she was only a girl, ultimately she would not count for much. From her mother, Anna heard, "Don't be sexy"; but she also heard that she should be someone special, probably a professional dancer as her

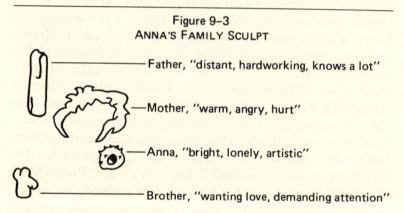

Figure 9–3
ANNA'S FAMILY SCULPT

Father, "distant, hardworking, knows a lot"

Mother, "warm, angry, hurt"

Anna, "bright, lonely, artistic"

Brother, "wanting love, demanding attention"

Messages.

From father: "I don't want you. Work hard, but you won't be successful."
From mother: "Be what I wanted to be (a dancer), but don't be sexy."
From brother: "Pay attention to me."
From Anna, to parents: "I'll work hard at being what you want, but I won't succeed and I won't be sexy."
From Anna to brother: "I'll pay attention to you rather than me."

mother had wanted to be. For a long time Anna took lessons, practiced, and struggled to become a dancer. It did not occur to her that she had combined, and was acting out, her parents' directives; a struggling, nonsexy dancer was certainly not going to count for much!

I work with the sculpt on three levels of analysis: first as a picture of the actual family in which the client grew up, the screens he developed for certain kinds of experience, and the decisions he made about who he was and how to make it in life; second, as clues to his projections upon other people in current life; and third, as a picture of his inner self, the internal programming with which he limits his options. When we have gotten through this, he rearranges the figures, not to cancel out anything but to bring different facets into relationship so that they now symbolize the self he is aiming to develop in therapy.

An intellectual exercise so far, but now the core injunctions were identified and could be used to re-experience early memories and the options that were not chosen and to trigger Bioenergetic exercises. The experiences and

---

Figure 9–4
ANNA'S SCULPT AS A PICTURE OF HER OWN SELF

Message.

"I choose to be me—not mother's idea of me; and that means connecting more with my body." Here she places the sculpt of herself, a head with spiky bumps, on top of the headless body of her infant brother sculpt. "I love to dance, though not professionally. I love to make things and use my hands, I haven't done this for years, but I choose to now."

"The strong masculine and the wounded feminine aspects in me make a good pair when they are related." Here she places the masculine tower within the crescent of the feminine. "I block myself when I keep them apart."

feelings that were blocked could be reconnected. For instance, in Anna's family it was forbidden to feel either sexy
or angry, so instead of appropriately experiencing those
forbidden feelings, Anna became sad and powerless, which
was acceptable and even stimulated some attention. After
initial work on breathing, I had her lie on a mattress and
kick, trying out words like, "I won't," "you can't make me."
She said the words over and over. Occasionally I inserted
one of the parental injuctions or pointed out when she was
holding her breath or how she was restricting her body,
until finally she exploded with the repressed rage.

We continued work with her sexual feelings. She
painted her own feelings as they now felt inside her body
and did another painting of the constriction she felt in
expressing them. I had her watch eight hours of the sexual
attitude restructuring films of the National Sexual Forum.
We continued body work, for example, breathing exercises, then lying on the mattress with feet and upper shoulders braced, lifting and letting fall her buttocks with the
phrase, "Look at me! Recognize me," until sexual feelings
were mobilized, which she painted, now integrating them
with elements from the two previous paintings. Her paintings deepened in feeling intensity. The paintings acted as
a container focusing and deepening the experience of her
sexuality as co-extensive with her wholeness, her whole
self.

In my experience, emotional flooding is most readily
achieved with a combination of body work and art, but
often the induction process which precedes this starts in a
different place. Work with Cassie, an ex-nun, provides an
example. Initially when I saw her she did little but weep.
The sessions contained long blank pauses and fairly accurately reflected the life she led. Living alone and working
at a bookkeeping job that in no way reflected her intellectual ability or academic achievements, she also took no
initiative in establishing a social life and rejected any at-

tempts by others to get to know her. I accepted her for treatment, but I felt inwardly exhausted when I thought of her passive anger, which needed to be identified and expressed. Her description of her past was for the most part as a victim of circumstances and other people's bad will. She was not in touch with her own actions, which beartrapped others into "doing the wrong thing," which she then judged as their fault and used to justify her victim role and immobility.

I was particularly pessimistic about the use of any art forms, as Cassie had previously drawn only scribbles or stick figures when I suggested this expression. About midway in her treatment, however, after she had made good use of symbolism in verbal fantasies, I decided to introduce this dimension by suggesting that we do a nonverbal dialogue with color crayons. I thought in this way to introduce her to the various ways the color stick could be used and

the kind of statements that could be made. I drew some teasing lines in the yellow, contradicting one of her strong black statements. Her response was immediate. She not only recognized the teasing but with a burst of spontaneous humor gave it back to me. She thereafter worked alone and drew some quite powerful feeling statements, indicating how much had been held in. She began to make use of fantasy and bibliotherapy materials.

I have clients type inner dialogues when they are becoming conscious of opposing feelings and thoughts emerging within. The exercise is to simply sit at a typewriter, write one sentence, listen, then write whatever comes to mind, continuing in dialogue fashion. Gradually, a picture emerges that can almost be specified as an inner group. Usually there is a crying child, a moralist, and a renegade of some sort as well as an objective observer. The aim is differentiation—awareness of the components of identity in order to achieve a more deeply integrated, firmer sense of the choosing ego who mediates the expression of these inner aspects. This is the beginning work with the elements of myth described in the third phase of the chart in Figure 2.

In her dialogues, Cassie identified a crying baby, a small, red, angry child, a critical analyst cum executioner, and a distinctly inept mediator. I had her paint them and fantasize their starting out on a journey together, what they would each bring, and how they would manage various obstacles. In this way she found that the crying baby actually had a very good feeling sense and knew what would meet her needs; the angry child was male, had independence, strength, and more than a streak of the adventurer in him; the critic was nasty but a very good computer

navigator and eventually even developed his own brand of vinegary humor. We now could look for where these strengths were in her.

I suggested she read Laurens van der Post's *Venture to the Interior,* a tale of an African safari that can also be read as a journey to the interior of the psyche, and Sheila Moon's *Knee Deep in Thunder,* which has a similar way of symbolizing instinctual aspects that have to be discovered, respected, and known. She went to the movie *Walkabout,* a story of an Australian aborigine who rescues and travels with a young woman and her brother—finally, not being really understood or seen, he dies. She recognized her situation in these art forms and saw that she had the option of either responding and using the newly discovered instinctual elements within her or letting them die. She did not let them die. In group session several months later, she pulled baby, red child, and computer navigator together and remarked casually to one of the men, "You really turn me on." He did. They have been comfortably married for several years now.

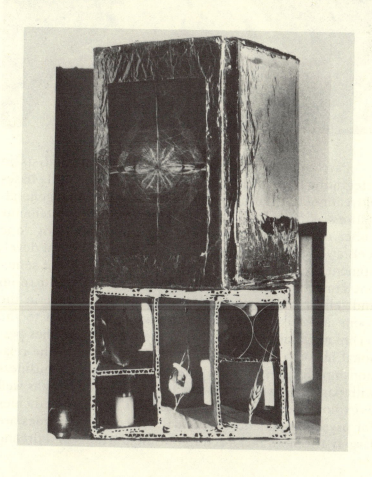

Psychodrama exercises can be powerful catalysts in integrating feeling with insight, and I use them in all phases of treatment. A standard rule to avoid impersonal generalizations is always to have the client use "I" statements rather than "one" or "you," "I felt awkward," not "one feels awkward in a situation. . . ." There is a natural development then in saying to a client who complains of someone's injustice, "Don't gossip; bring him/her into the room and tell him how you feel." Imagining the other in the room and talking to him is an easy introduction to the technique. Making the past into the present revivifies personal history. Painting the feelings contained in the relationships focuses and deepens them. Unfinished business with parents, saying good-bye to past relationships as well as exploring options and other endings, are natural themes for psychodrama and art. Actually, Gestalt techniques are largely Psychodrama—acting out the portions of a dream, giving a voice to exaggerated body movements, and so on. I usually precede a Psychodrama session with some body movement work, either relaxation exercises from behavior modification as developed by Wolpe and Lazarus or bioenergetic techniques I learned from Alexander Lowen and Stanley Keleman.

I will conclude this section with a client's description of what she learned on her fifth day of treatment, but first I will describe it as I experienced it. The episode included all phases of the loss-grieving cycle. Sandra, a forty-four-

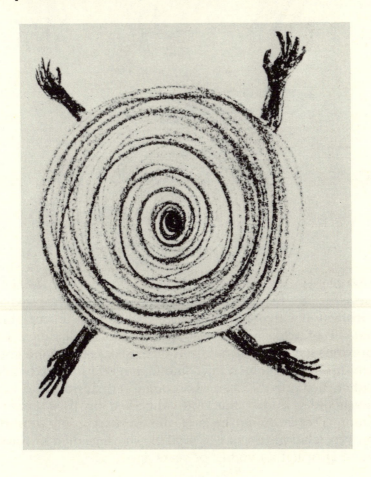

year-old woman, was referred to me by one of my psychiatric associates because of her inability to experience sexual satisfaction with her husband. She had done a considerable amount of work and experienced a peak of exhilaration the previous day when she realized she had expressed and gotten through the anger, hurt, and loss in relationship to her father, her only brother who committed suicide, and her much older former husband, who died on their honeymoon. This morning she knew that we were going to work on her relationship to her mother who had died in Napa State Hospital a number of years ago.

Sandra's mood was clearly depressed. She expressed the reservations and pessimism she felt. I had her start with Keleman's anger-releasing kicking exercises, but it was clear she could not get in tune with any of this. She stated that her mother had been so good to her; she had been the mother's whole life. She said mother couldn't help what she was; she was weak. She didn't know anything about sex herself, so how could she be expected to help her daughter? Mother had never expressed any anger toward Sandra. They had slept together in the same bed throughout her childhood. Sandra could not even spend a night away from

home without becoming unbearably homesick. She was twenty-seven before she broke away, and even then the separation was difficult.

It was obvious to me that Sandra had to recognize the suffocating, smothering quality in her mother's love. She inwardly knew this and had, in fact, freed herself physically —but not emotionally, because she did not recognize that her existence was threatened. I suggested that she lie on the floor; I covered her with a blanket and several large pillows. I then lay on top of this and pinned her down. Acting the voice of her mother, I then began a monologue sweetly, gently, saying, "I will always be with you. You are my precious child. I sacrificed my life for you, but it was worthwhile because as long as you live, I will live too because I will always be with you."

Sandra's reaction is described in this excerpt from her journal.

> My mother died today, and I don't feel sad, nor am I even able to shed a tear for her. I have a feeling of great relief and release because I have finally been able to break her very strong hold on me. I have fought her and won.
> When Margaret began today, I thought it was just a game. I really didn't know what she had in mind, but I wasn't afraid. When I began to feel uncomfortable under the blanket I put up a small effort to get out. Then I began to feel I was going to suffocate and become terribly afraid. I called out to Margaret, rather than my mother, thinking Margaret would see I was in trouble and get off. She didn't and went on acting as my mother smothering me with her love and need for me. It was when I realized that Margaret wasn't going to let me escape from reality, like I'd always done, and that I was going to have to fight my way out, I screamed. It was a terrible feeling of panic and fear, and I knew I had to fight to get out—that I just couldn't give up.
> After, I realized that that was the only way I could get away from my mother—with a violent effort. I never could have argued or reasoned my way from her. . . . It wasn't until I had this life and death struggle on the floor that I could admit

my anger and my resentment. She had tried to take my life from me, tried to kill me as a person just as surely as if she had tried to suffocate me. I had to fight this life and death struggle, because it was my life she was taking, had been taking for years and was still taking even from her grave. . . . I feel now that I am free of her and that I can have my own needs and desires, and no longer carry that guilty feeling I have always had about her. . . . The way her life turned out was not my doing in any way—her troubles began long before I was even born.

I know now that I could never be a whole person as long as she was still there. . . . I had a great feeling of despair yesterday when I thought the task of freeing myself from my mother was impossible. It was like a great brick wall in my path. I had come so far and then came up against this high wall. Today I knocked the wall down and can proceed on the path my own way and nobody else's.

I thought of Andrew on the way home and realized that I had never really let him in. I've never let him know my true feelings, and I think now that it is because I have been afraid that if I did, he would have a power over me, like Mother did. . . . Now that I realize that I have my own needs and desires and that they are valid ones, I don't have to fear letting Andrew in. I can tell him my true feelings without being afraid of losing my own identity. I am entitled to these feelings, just as much as he is entitled to his.

The sad feeling and tears I had when thinking of my father were mostly for me, because I was cheated and never really had a father. The tears for my brother were for him and because I realized how it was nearly me that ended that way —how it could have been me. I had no tears for Robert or my mother. I am glad to see them go.

I don't know how this new feeling of mine will work out in terms of Andrew's and my sex life, but I feel I would like us to begin again . . . This feeling of rebirth in my life should be carried through in all my experiences . . . experimenting with the sense of feeling, getting to know one another and what sensations please—We have never really done this, never really learned about one another in this way.

The period of intensive daily treatment characteristi-cally releases a significant increase of energy and a subjective sense of well-being, undoubtedly a function of feeling really listened to; but there is also a sense of having found and recovered parts of the self which now want to be cared for and developed. There is a tentativeness and sense of vulnerability with the newness, but this is felt as a good way to be, in touch with the growing edges. It is a vulnerable time, and there is particular need for close follow-up in the next months.

In addition to its value in individual psychotherapy, art is also a viable medium in group work. Before this stage, however, I find that Videotaping can be an effective adjunct to group treatment in the initial session when group members are characteristically interacting from their persona roles. The camera focuses not only upon the person speaking but on listeners' affective responses in body movement and expression. Also, selected replay can plug into the tensions for subsequent Gestalt work. Another use is with the inner-theater design of dreams and Psychodrama. The group member working with a dream describes the characters and the setting and selects group members to enact each part. He then tells the dream and we extemporize, playing the dream onward. I encourage group members to embody the descriptive adjectives and to exaggerate the direction of each part. The dreamer as author and director can interrupt at any point, suggests a different slant, or play a particular part until the issues in the dream clarify and move toward closure. The players identify their own life experiences, which reflect into the parts.

As for art itself, creating his own work not only facilitates contact with the client's unknown inner aspects, it also enables their integration—particularly of the despised, disliked aspects of self. For example, during the judiciary committee hearings on Watergate I was working with a group of ministers and had each member make a list of adjectives or phrases describing the man or men on the committee who aroused their most negative feelings. I suggested that they add to their lists the characteristics of a person in their profession who for them epitomized the charlatan or false prophet—in Jungian terms, the shadow archetype of the healer or helping professional. Each then painted the composite of his or her adjectives and, meeting in small groups, each in turn described his painting in Gestalt fashion, identifying with it in the first person, present tense, active voice —for example, "I'm utterly ruthless. I don't care who or what gets in my way." "I'm a master manipulator with a million ways of rationalizing my actions." The groups had reached a point of trust that allowed the members to explore and sense what in them did in fact carry some of these attributes. Resistance was strong, as it always is in encountering the negative shadow archetype, but energy opened up as the projections were owned.

Another beginning exercise for groups, along with the family sculpt described earlier, is the construction of a self box, a three-dimensional accretion of some sort, not necessarily a box, but having an inside and an outer surface that is used in a meditative way to show what the person keeps on the inside and what outside as an official image. One woman constructed her box entirely of mirrors on the outside, indicating that she had always given everyone what they wanted to see. When it opened, however, the box fell completely apart; it had dark, nonhuman, crawling forms on the inside. Describing herself as the box, she wept as she spoke of the inner despair and isolation she felt, the suicide she considered.

Painting dreams for group therapy is much the same as it is in individual therapy, except that I encourage comments on another's work to be made grammatically only in the first person, present tense, active voice, in order to acknowledge projections and to allow the painter greater freedom to accept or reject a particular point of view. Painting feelings, the inner and outer aspects of felt conflicts, particularly for women involved in power issues, develops strong feeling. Finding some way to reconcile the elements of each into a third picture often taps a creative symbolic source which the verbal sharing in group helps to make explicit, and which leads to practical possibilities of resolution. Questions such as, "What new element have you introduced into the intregation painting? Does this correspond to anything in your real life?" are helpful.

Within a group or with couples, dialogue painting in silence facilitates the expression of tension in relationships. With couples, the two work on one painting. Competition, aggression, hesitancy, liking, relatedness, feelings that haven't been talked about, come quickly to the surface. The interacting couple share their responses first, then the group comments. The emphasis is on feeling issues in the here and now.

Painting the circular mandala always involves the reconciliation of opposites—the classic problem of squaring the circle. Emotional flooding it is not, for it develops best in a slow, carefully meditative way after the polarized affect has been identified and worked with. This is an integrative technique that strengthens the possibility of owning and living with new feelings, new aspects of the self that initially felt too threatening or too foreign to the familiar known self.

Art offers many possibilities for trying out new growth. An example is the following exercise for getting women into deeper touch with aspects of their femininity that have not yet developed.

Jungian psychology postulates that within the feminine experience are specific styles of being, of awareness; ways of relating to reality, digesting it, and making judgments. These modalities express themselves in their own characteristic images, behavior patterns, and emotional responses. Jung reasons that as we grow to wholeness and struggle to overcome the opposition within ourselves, we begin an endless process of reconciling our indwelling op-

posites and polarities. Out of a series of successive reconcil-
iations, the self is gradually constructed. In helping women
to differentiate and develop their own feminine consciousness and experience, I use the paradigm of Toni Wolf for
the polarities of the feminine—mother, hetaira, amazon,
and medial woman. The woman who primarily functions as
need-responding mother either is helping or devouring,
nourishing or being a martyr. She usually projects much of
her unlived life onto her son. The hetaira, or anima, woman
tends to submerge her own identity into that of her man.
She becomes what she senses he expects her to be. The
amazon has a virginal quality of self-containment, can be
cold, but has a well-developed ego and functions primarily
as a comrade to man. The medial woman, or Sophia figure,
wise woman or witch, displays a firm ego and can be highly
discriminating but functions primarily in relation to man as
a mediator for the unconscious.

In helping women to connect with this rather abstract
formulation, I first have them identify the primary relationships they have and have had with men, how they felt about
them, what they wanted. I encourage them to look through
the heap of magazines I provide for images, symbols that
express aspects of their relationships, and then to select
those which seem most central and begin gluing them into
a collage. I encourage them to paint over the collage in
order to develop and emphasize perceived themes. When
finished, and when discussion has deepened an awareness
of the primary type, I have them pair up with one or more
of an opposite type. Alternately, they ask the questions:
"Who are you? What do you want?" and listen without
comment. When this is finished, each works alone to
deepen her awareness of the type of woman she least identifies with, then in art form with paint or clay begins to
depict what this repressed or embryonic part of her feels
like and wants to have happen. This can have a powerful
"birthing" effect.

In my experiences with clients, I find there are specifically feminine styles of being, of awareness, and of relatedness. These styles are also available to men and can be discovered and integrated in the process of treatment even as women can discover and claim their masculine potentials for self-assertion. Therefore, in designing treatment I do not use different methods for men and women. The choice of art process evolves in the context of each individual exploring and discovering his or her own experience. The examples used illustrate problems women commonly bring to therapy: depression, lack of sexual satisfaction, poor self-concept and body image, a sense of powerlessness— but for each of these I could add a masculine example.

The use of art allows the personal, highly individual image and symbol to emerge from the inner growing edge of self. It develops and contains feeling responses until they can be known and allowed their place within a more inclusive sense of self. It functions both to stimulate emotional flooding and also to contain, connect, integrate, and transform powerful polarities as they are uncovered in intensive daily treatment. The inclusion of art media is one facet in a total design of treatment.

PART III

The following chapters focus primarily upon the direct stimulation of affect as practiced by representatives of what might loosely be termed the cognitively oriented modalities. The term is meant to encompass those psychotherapists who largely, or exclusively, rely upon verbal interchanges with their patients.

As will be seen, a great many verbal, nonaction techniques are successful in releasing emotion within a rather conventional psychotherapeutic or even psychoanalytic setting if the therapist is willing to experiment or bend time-honored rules. Often these newer cognitive methods are systematic components of an entire psychoanalysis, fitted to particular patients. They are also used in specific situations —for example, in the context of pathological mourning. But however they are employed, they have enriched and broadened the scope of what has come to be called "talk-therapy."

chapter 10

RE-GRIEF THERAPY AND THE FUNCTION OF THE LINKING OBJECT AS A KEY TO STIMULATE EMOTIONALITY

Vamik D. Volkan, M.D.
Anthony F. Cilluffo, Ph.D.
Thomas L. Sarvay, Jr., M.D.

Re-grief therapy (Volkan 1966, 1968, 1971, in press) is designed for the adult patient who has become established in a pattern of pathological response to the death of an intimate, loved/hated figure. Its psychotherapeutic maneuvers thaw emotions which, in the case of such people, are "frozen" rather than running a normal course and becoming attenuated to a manageable sadness. This thawing process in re-grief therapy is facilitated by the use of "linking objects." These are objects typically treasured by people unable to resolve their grief—something that magically provides the illusion of communication with the dead. The pathological mourner can control this illusory communication, turning it on by musing over the object and turning it off by putting the object out of sight in an accessible place. Thus he can either recall the dead person or reject (kill) him in a pattern that reflects the ambivalent relationship of the past. The heavy emotional investment the mourner makes in such an object makes it a key with which to unlock the emotionality that then becomes manageable and even healing when the reasons for the previous failure to grieve are identified and both the emotionality experienced and the interpretations that accompany it are brought under the scrutiny of the patient's observing ego.

Adult Reactions to Death

The patterns we have seen in our study of adult reactions to death, grief, and re-griefing at the University of Virginia are consistent with what many others have reported as grief reactions of adults who have lost a loved/-hated intimate. Kübler-Ross (1969) offers a similar pattern and applies it also to the person who knowingly awaits his own death. Engel (1961) suggests a comparison between the process of grieving and the healing of a wound, which is predictably accomplished in the absence of contamination but seriously compromised by infection.

Volkan (1972a, 1974) identified at least six preconditions that can complicate (infect) the grieving/healing process. They occur in either of two sets of circumstances: (1) when the death occurred so suddenly that the mourner's ego perceives it as a trauma he cannot work through without help, and something like a traumatic neurosis results; or (2) when the mourner had been both extremely dependent on and highly ambivalent toward the one who died and had "unfinished business" with him. Such ambivalent or even hostile dependency can stem from unfinished business from any level of psychosexual development (Volkan 1970, 1972a, 1974). Thus, psychologically, the patient cannot permit the dead person to disappear; he is needed to resolve previously unfinished conflicts. Although intellectually aware that his intimate other is indeed dead, he avails himself of a splitting mechanism (Freud 1938) to reassure himself without developing a psychosis that this is not the case after all and that the one he has in fact lost is still accessible to him. It is usual for these two factors to come into play together and to make varying contributions to the patient's general condition.

In spite of semantic and theoretical differences, investigators generally agree that one responds to the death of a significant other by shock, denial, anger, and an effort to bargain for escape from the tragedy, along with a hope that the dead will somehow return. These responses, along with the disorganization that ensues, are characteristic of the grieving process, from which evolves a gradually more realistic acceptance of loss, a growing independence from the intrapsychic representation of the dead, and ultimate investment in new objects.

How long can grief continue and still be considered "normal"? It is a complex and time-consuming process which, in the end, leads to adaptation of "the internal psychic milieu to an altered external milieu" (Pollack 1961); but there are individual differences from mourner to mourner in its course. Our studies have led us to believe that although normal grief may last for a year or two it follows a progressive course in which acute symptoms—that is, anger, diffused or focused, and a search for the dead sufficiently obsessive to disrupt daily life, strong preoccupation with feelings of guilt, and somatic distress—lessen or disappear within six months.

Established Pathological Mourning

The person suffering from established pathological mourning usually freezes at the stage Bowlby and Parkes

(1970) refer to as "the yearning to recover the lost object." This stage is pathological when characterized by a concomitant dread of finding him that reflects the ambivalence with which the mourner had regarded the dead individual in life. The clinical diagnosis of "established pathological mourning" is justified when these contradictory forces remain effective six months after the death. The preoccupation with this dual possibility may be chronic and disrupt the patient's daily life for years, or it may surface with dramatic force on the anniversary of the death. One of our patients, for example, had changed his wife's burial place three times in as many years, and when he came into treatment he was about to change it once more in his preoccupation with the thought of her not being happy with his choice. Another dreamt at least three times a week for four years after his father died that the corpse, which showed no sign of decay, lay before him; he would awaken from this dream gripped by anxiety. The subject of reincarnation fascinates such mourners. One patient, fully aware that his father had been dead for years, was so struck by a resemblance he saw in the face of a passing stranger that he had to pursue the stranger and peer into his face to make certain that it was not his father returned to life. Such mourners usually use the present tense when they speak of the ones they have lost. They often deny the existence of a grave, and if they are responsible for securing a tombstone, they may fail to make the appropriate arrangements.

Certain dreams are typical for the pathological mourner. Volkan (1970, 1971, 1974) identified two that are common. In one, the dead individual, usually undisguised, is engaged in a life-and-death struggle from which the mourner tries to rescue him by efforts thwarted each time by his awakening from sleep. These dreams are repeated, and their invevitably inconclusive ending reflects the unfinished business of grieving. Other dreams are motionless tableaux, typically described by the dreamer as "frozen," in a reflection of his fixation (freezing) at one point in the grieving process. There may be a sequence of such tableaux, but although one may follow another, there is no motion within any one of them.

The clinical picture is dominated by direct or symbolic preoccupation with the dead person, and the simultaneous desire and dread concerning reunion with him. However, the patient's condition can best be assessed by an examination of his dynamic intrapsychic processes, especially when covering defensive maneuvers are established to deal with the anxiety of the wish for reunion and dread of it. Such processes may, for the sake of simplicity, be divided into two groups: (1) internalization processes and (2) externalization processes.

THE INTROJECT AND INTERNALIZATION PROCESSES. Abraham (1911) and Freud (1917) brought the internalization processes (introjection, identification) to our attention in their studies of the psychodynamics of mourning and melancholia. When the search for the lost one forces the mourner to test the reality of his disappearance, he uses hundreds of memories to bind him to the person he has lost and becomes so preoccupied with them that he loses interest in the world around him. His painful longing must be worked through by surrendering the dead individual piecemeal, as though he were composed of one memory after another, and tension is discharged through weeping. Communication with the dead is also maintained by the mechanism of introjection. The dead person is "taken in," and thus the dead individual's representation (introject) within the patient's self becomes hypertrophied. Psychoanalysis has long suggested that it is easier to loosen a tie with one's introject than to loosen one's ties with an external object

presumably because in this case our inner world is more tractable than the world around us. Thus introjections [in-

trojects] act as a buffer by helping to preserve the relationship with the object while the gradual process of
relinquishing is going on. [Fenichel 1945]

One then expects that when the work of mourning is
concluded the representation of the dead individual will
retreat to a level at which it no longer demands constant
relatedness with the patient's self and at which the patient
no longer is ambivalently dependent upon it. Part of the
introject could be carried along to the next step of identification in which, in the case of uncomplicated mourning, the
mourner identifies himself with the functional adaptive aspects of the departed. Two courses of internalization may
occur when the relationship with the introject remains ambivalent and disruptive. Either the mourner may identify
totally with the introject, in which case boundaries between
the dead person's representation and the patient's self-
representation may melt away and the relationship with the
dead become an altogether intrapsychic process so that the
patient relates to himself with destructive ambivalence,
presenting the clinical picture of a reactive depressive reaction, or the mourner keeps the introject within his breast
as if it were in effect a foreign body, and, in spite of the
internal locus of this process, relates to the representation
of the dead as though it existed independently. Such a
patient may tell how he has carried on conversations for
years with the dead person who lives on in his bosom. Such
a relationship is disruptive, and the patient may at times
show an urgent necessity to rid himself of his invisible
companion; he may even cry in anger, "Get out!" The
clinical picture in such cases is one of established pathological mourning.

It should be remembered that although an introject
can effect identification as though its borderlines melted
away, identification itself remains capable of moving in reverse; the partner in identification may reappear as an introject. Thus, established depressive reactions after a death

and established pathological mourning are closely related. If we see that identifications can easily attain introject status, we accept the patient for "re-griefing," as will be explained.

A young, happily married physician came into treatment with the complaint that he had suddenly turned into a Don Juan and his behavior, which was accompanied by depressive feelings, was jeopardizing his marriage. He was unable to understand what had made him desert his better judgment during the past two years. It was revealed that his younger brother had been killed in an automobile accident two years earlier. He had been a handsome youth, widely known for his conquests, and he had been buried with his Playboy Club membership card in his hand. There had been considerable comment at the funeral about his amorous feats and the tragedy of his aborted career as a lover. It was then evident that our patient had totally identified himself with his brother and that it was with this identification that he was philandering. With this insight, the patient experienced a change of symptoms. He now complained that although he himself had the urge to go after women it was the brother he carried within him who enforced his orders that he do so. The brother's image had become an introject.

Total identification in the pathological mourner is accomplished only by a merging in which the representation of the dead fuses with that of the mourner and the latter suddenly starts behaving like the one he mourns. By this process of merging, total identification is temporarily achieved without the process of an introject's turning into an identification. This manifestation may appear in something as relatively undramatic as gestures that had characterized the dead individual, and it may be quite transient.

THE LINKING OBJECT AND THE PROCESSES OF EXTERNALIZATION. Volkan (1972*a*, 1972*b*, 1974, in press) observed that our pathological mourners at the University of Virginia had each adopted something that he used in a magical way to deal with his loss. People often cling to keepsakes of the dead or souvenirs of past relationships, but they are likely to put them to appropriate use and in any case seldom regard them as having eerie powers of their own. The established pathological mourner, however, feels a kind of taboo about wearing or using his keepsake and guards it jealously. It exerts a spell over him. Since such objects link the mourner with the one he mourns, and symbolize the bond of love/hate between them, they are well called linking objects.

The linking object is chosen from among:

1. The belongings of the dead—sometimes something he wore, such as a watch.

2. Things the dead person once used as an extension of his senses, such as a camera (an extension of seeing).

3. Symbolic or realistic representations of the dead person, the simplest example of which would be a photograph.

4. Things at hand when the news of death was received or when the mourner saw the body. These we call "last-minute objects," since they recall the last moment during which the full impact of the living personality of the other was available. For example, one patient received word of his brother's accidental death just as he was sitting down to play a stack of phonograph records, and these became his linking objects.

One patient, Julia, had as a linking object a red robe of her own that her mother wore constantly during her last months. This patient, a single woman, was in her thirties at the time of her mother's death, and although she realized intellectually that her mother was no longer living, her behavior denied the fact. She yearned for her mother's return but dreaded it also.

Julia was the youngest of six. The mother had been severely burned when her last child was six months old. Bedridden for a year, the mother had been unable to carry out her mothering functions. The early mother-daughter relationship, which contained elements of unresolved separation-individuation (Mahler 1968), manifested itself in later years as sadomasochistic. Although her siblings left home, the patient stayed with the mother, who was widowed and, during the last ten years of her life, an amputee because of diabetes. Julia had surrendered all independent social life, a college scholarship, and opportunities for marriage to care for her mother. Although she sometimes wished for her mother's death, she kept in touch with her day and night at regular intervals "to see if she was all right," phoning her from work several times daily, sleeping at the foot of her bed and checking periodically during the night.

After the mother died she appeared often in her daughter's dreams and fantasies, clad in the red robe in which she had died. Julia had purchased it for herself on one of her infrequent holidays but gave it to her mother at her request. It became a linking object, an ambivalence-strained link that had to be externalized and put aside. The daughter became actually afraid of it and took pains to avoid contact with it. A summary of her re-grief therapy appears later.

Volkan's study (1972b) of the linking object persuaded him that it provides an external locus in which part of the patient's projected self-representation may meet externally with part of the projected object representation of the deceased individual. This meeting provides a link in which the ambivalent object relationship is not renounced but "frozen." Although great care may be taken to keep it out of sight, it is important to know where it is at any given moment. The ambivalence of wanting to annihilate the deceased and simultaneously longing for him is condensed in it, and it provides an external reference for the painful and unresolved work of mourning. For example, his dead father's photograph in a folder became a linking object for Mike (Volkan 1971). He put the photograph under a leaking pipe "by accident." In his fantasy the folder represented the coffin containing the father, and he was afraid to open it. When he finally did so during his re-grief therapy, it was with emotional outpouring. The act of keeping the photograph under the water represented his attempt to "kill" his father (to complete grieving), since his father had died after snorkeling in the sea. Further associations indicated, however, that the dripping water represented the tears he had been unable to shed over his dead father. When an understanding of this came to the patient's awareness during his treatment he broke into sobs. Thus it can be seen how the linking object enables internalized object relationships with the dead to be externally maintained.

One of the most interesting ramifications of the linking object concept is the combining of parts of projected self-and-object representations within it. The kind of introject earlier described as pertaining to established pathological mourning serves much the same purpose; from the point of view of the patient the foreign body in his bosom is a locus—this time an internal one—in which self-and-object representations can meet. It should be remembered that it is the patient who perceives the introject as a concrete inner presence. The therapist must keep in mind that this presence is laden with considerable affect and many unconscious dynamic forces. The linking object holds magic for the patient only; the therapist will find it a key to use in treatment only when he interprets what is condensed in it.

With the exception of transient experiences of merging with the dead one, the established pathological mourner's main inner link with him is through the introject, and the outer link with him is through the linking object.

THE SELECTION OF PATIENTS FOR RE-GRIEF THERAPY

Candidates for re-grief work are chosen from among adult patients suffering from "established pathological mourning" after each has been evaluated, a formulation accounting for his inability to grieve at the "normal" time made, and his tolerance of anxiety and sadness assessed. Since the death of an adult's intimate other reactivates feelings and attitudes from the past, special attention should be given to any losses the patient experienced in his childhood and to his handling of them as well as his response to the loss of intrapsychic separation from the mother during childhood.

The established pathological mourner has regressed to the employment of early defense mechanisms such as denial, introjection, projection, somatization, and the maintenance of control over his psychic distance from the external object. The patient who had been fixated at the level where such defenses are used before undergoing his recent loss is not suitable for re-griefing; nor is the individual with narcissistic character pathology, although the latter may present symptoms of chronic pathological mourning because of the inability of his narcissistic core to let anyone who is idealized go. The occurrence of death may initiate pathological mourning that can be so overlaid with defenses as to change the clinical picture to one of some other established neurosis or even a psychosomatic or psychotic condition; when this occurs the clinical condition determines the appropriate treatment. On the other hand, in a brief examinition of the issues with the patient one should assess the possibilities of turning an established neurotic condition precipitated by death into typical established pathological mourning. We already described how a patient's neurotic depressive reaction with Don Juan symptomatology revealed an underlying established state of pathological mourning. In the case of Clyde, to be described, the surface manifestations suggested schizophrenia but the initial evaluation was set aside when a diagnosis of established pathological mourning was made.

In the diagnosis of established pathological mourning it should be distinguished from three other clinical conditions in particular. These are (1) depression, which has similar but not identical internalization processes; (2) fetishism, which involves the investment of inanimate objects with special properties but in which the object (fetish) is used by the adult to deal primarily with castration anxiety and only secondarily with separation anxiety, unlike the linking object, which deals with separation anxiety evoked by a death; and (3) schizophrenia, which shares the break with reality but in which the break is not focal and circumscribed as it is in pathological mourning nor as buffered by the use of splitting, which serves the mourner as a protection against a generalized break with reality (psychosis).

Our psychologist (Cilluffo) showed that the Minnesota Multiphasic Personality Inventory (MMPI) was not only an effective self-rating measurement of change that took place during re-grief therapy but that it offered promise for the selection of patients for this type of treatment. Patients diagnosed as pathological mourners and successfully treated by re-griefing generally demonstrated underlying personality traits of hysteria and dependence. A pilot study suggested that established pathological mourners tended to show an elevation of scales 1, 2, 3, 7, and 8, and, to a lesser extent, of scales 4 and 6. Peaks generally came in scales 2 and 7, and the pilot data suggest that elevation of scales 2 and 7 to a point in excess of the showing on scale

8 is predictive of maximum benefit from re-griefing. This research study also provided evidence that there is an increase in emotionality in the first part of re-grief therapy which is then resolved in the latter stages of treatment.

A Descriptive Account of Re-grief Therapy

Once the diagnosis is made, the patient is told that his psychological condition has been precipitated by the death of his intimate other and that he has not completed the grieving process. The goal of the therapy to be given is limited to two specific outcomes. He is to be helped to understand why he has not in the past been able to complete his grieving, and he is then to be assisted to complete it in the present, to experience and to express the emotions generated by his loss. It is explained that therapy will terminate when he can feel relief from his load and let the dead person rest in peace, and that he will thereafter be able to invest himself more freely in new objects.

Since the established pathological mourner is in a state of chronic hope (Volkan 1970) that the dead will return and simultaneously gripped by dread at the prospect of such reunion, he is helped during the first phase of re-grief therapy to make distinctions between what actually belongs to him and what actually belongs to the one he has lost. Volkan and Showalter (1968) have referred to this initial treatment phase as the demarcation phase. At this time the patient is in a "state of contact" with the dead individual—internally, by keeping the introject of him and externally, through a linking object. The taking of a detailed history initiates the building of boundaries between the patient and the representation of the dead at these contact points. We conduct our history taking in a nondirective exchange and then arrive at a formulation as to why the patient would not allow the dead person to die. The therapist uses his findings in his later interpretations. In the initial phase, we may ask the patient to bring a picture of a dead person (not a linking object) and ask him to look at it and to describe the appearance of its subject. We do this to foster a focused consideration of the dead individual and further differentiation, at least on the intellectual level, between him and the patient himself.

The circumstances of the death that afflicted the patient are carefully examined. An example of the relevance of such probing is furnished by a woman patient in her late thirties who had lost her son in an automobile accident. Her grieving process started normally enough, but was complicated by the arrival within a week of a younger sister who was leaving her husband because he accused her of having an affair with the patient's husband. The patient had always assumed the role of a protective elder sister toward her sibling, and this involvement aborted the progress of the grieving process, as we were able to interpret to her two years later. It is usual for male patients who are only sons or the eldest son at home when the father died during their teen years to report that other family members had promptly turned to them as the head of the household but at the same time regarded them as children to be protected from the grim circumstances that attend death and burial.

We see the patient often, usually three or four times a week, in order to emphasize the intensity and continuity of the processes our treatment puts in train. The whole course of the treatment takes an average time of three months. This form of therapy does not rely on the development and resolution of a transference neurosis; but transference manifestations do, of course, take place, and throughout the treatment we interpret them, prematurely as we know, in order to abort the development of a full-fledged transference neurosis. Rado (1956) uses the term "interceptive interpretation," which we have modified to our purpose in describing our interception of the development of transference neurosis as it occurs in long-term insight therapies.

When the therapist observes the patient viewing him, either symbolically or openly, as the dead father, he verbalizes to the patient his awareness of this "transference," and the fact that he is someone other than the father.

After the initial phase of treatment, which usually lasts several weeks, the therapist focuses on the patient's linking objects and their use. These open the way for the patient to experience emotional storms and to observe the reasons for them. The achievement of the ability to so express and observe—and to experience the grief process postponed from the time of the death—is at the heart of this type of therapy.

The therapist must sometimes help the patient identify his linking object. He may begin by asking, "What kind of special token of———do you keep?" The patient may acknowledge to himself his use of a linking object, but he is likely to point to something so highly symbolized that its meaning is not altogether clear to him. The therapist will then formulate the reasons for the choice of this particular object, which may condense different aspects of the patient's reaction to his loss.

For example, a young man chose as his linking object a handkerchief taken from among his father's belongings immediately after his father died. In the course of a hundred hours of treatment, it became clear that many circumstances in his life had dictated this choice. His mother had been openly unfaithful to her husband four years before he died, and he had responded to the situation by a daily recitation of the Shakespearean scene in which Othello murders Desdemona, crying, "Fetch me that handkerchief!" in reference to the token of supposed unfaithfulness. Since his mother had been seductive toward him, the handkerchief became a link between the "incestuous" patient and his "oedipal" father. During the last years of his life, the father had for some reason used a handkerchief so constantly that it became his trademark. The patient had been injured some years before and had lost a testicle in consequence. After his father died, the young man impulsively looked under the deathbed—an action understood only in subsequent therapy, which disclosed his wish that the father had left him one of his testicles. The handkerchief represented in this connection his empty scrotum awaiting this gift. When the patient was five he had been hospitalized and thus separated from his mother. When a little girl in the next bed died, the stains on her bedsheets left a lasting impression on his mind in connection with separation and death, and the handkerchief reproduced this symbolism. Since the handkerchief is used when one weeps, the control he had over his handkerchief—being able to put it out of sight—gave him the illusion that he could control the grieving process.

Knowledge of what is condensed in the linking object of his patient helps the therapist make interpretations to loosen the points of contact between the patient's self-representation and the representation of the dead person. The linking object also serves to show the patient how his grieving has an external reference as though it were entirely exterior to his inner experience. The therapist must on no account be caught up in the patient's illusions about his linking objects, which are magical only in the patient's eyes.

In the next step in therapy, frozen emotions are stimulated and reawakened. It is quite possible that emotions may begin thawing before the linking object is introduced. Some patients seem to have been waiting for years to start crying and complete their grieving, and their emotions pour out as soon as the therapy is under way. When the patient is asked to bring his linking object to his sessions with the therapist, he invariably shuns looking closely at it or holding it, and the therapist does not insist that he do so until he seems to be ready. The therapist offers to keep the magical object in his office, since most patients are unwilling to carry a linking object to and from their therapeutic sessions and thus come into close contact with it. The patient is, however, given reassurance that it will be returned to him when it has lost its magical power and the patient himself wants it back. Some patients bring the object in a bag or briefcase to many sessions before they take it out. If the therapy is going well, they experience a flood of emotion as they finally take it in their hands. The tension then runs high; we have had patients who at this point ran screaming from the interview room. The first flood of emotions is diffuse, giving way to more and more differentiation, until the patient can name an emotion such as anger. The therapist, by now acquainted with the full range of the patient's reasons for withholding himself from grief, may help him to differentiate among his emotions and to identify such feelings as anger at the dead, narcissistic rage over being left behind, the fear of his own death, guilt over not having done right by the dead, and—in the end—sadness. The many shades of meaning in the relationship between the patient and the one he mourns are interpreted.

Emotional storms may continue for as long as several weeks. Now the therapist is more active in making his patient review the circumstances that attended the death—the place of death, his own reaction to the news, his reaction to viewing or not viewing the dead body, events that took place at the funeral. Two of our patients, without any suggestion from us, took a series of pictures that began at the funeral home and ended at the gravesite in order to relive the funeral in sessions with the therapist, and this time to relive it with appropriate emotion. One patient at this point gathered his family together for a memorial service for his dead brother. Many seek out their ministers or rabbis at this time to go into the meaning of funeral rites with them.

We try to determine when the patient's splitting began. One patient told us, for example, that as he gazed on the body he knew to be dead he saw it breathe. One may expect disorganization when the genesis of splitting has been identified and emotions stimulated by the use of linking objects before events have begun to come under secondary process consideration. The patient may consciously experience the not-reality-oriented aspect of his split ego functioning, believing briefly, for example, that the dead person is alive and searching for him more vigorously than before. The MMPI taken at this phase of re-griefing may actually show an increase on scale 8 as well as 2. This occurred in several cases in our pilot study and offers support for these clinical findings. The therapist continues to interpret the specific reasons the patient in question had to keep the dead alive and enables the patient to see that he needed something from the dead individual or that the dead person represented a part of himself. Since most such patients have never visited the grave they are asked, as a firmer reorganization takes place, to do so, examining their feelings and thoughts at the same time. Then they are encouraged to have a tombstone set in place if they are responsible for this but, denying the death, have failed to do so, as is often the case. When the re-griefing is over, the patient feels full of new energy and actively seeks new investments.

Throughout re-grief therapy the patient is encouraged to examine the manifest content of his dreams and fantasies. As therapy proceeds, such typical dreams as have been described give way to dreams in which the dreamer "kills" the one he has lost, if only by seeing the dead body as a form from which all sparks of life have gone forever.

Re-grief Work Applied

JULIA.   The therapy of Julia (treated by Volkan) whose use of a red robe as a linking object has been described, along with a brief review of her history, is summarized in what follows.

A contract was made with her for goal-limited brief psychotherapy, and thirty therapeutic sessions took place within a relatively short time, less than a month and a half. During this time she was an inpatient in a psychiatric ward. She was told that she had not completed the work of grieving and the goal of her therapy was to help her do so. Her first concern was her disturbing dreams, in one of which her mother lay in her coffin attempting to get out of it. The daughter then dreamed of calling the undertaker to give the mother "a shot of something to calm her down." She complained, "These dreams are killing me!" and the therapist was able to interpret her conflictual feelings, torn between wanting to keep her mother alive and wanting to "kill" her.

At the time of her mother's death, Julia had been "protected" by sympathetic friends and relatives from facing the reality of her loss. All of her mother's clothing, photographs, and other belongings had been removed from their home or hidden to spare her. She had not viewed the corpse, and she fainted at the funeral as she approached the coffin. She left the cemetery before the casket was lowered. All of these evasions fortified denial of her loss and supported the splitting mechanism.

Julia complained of weakness in her legs and difficulty in walking, recalling her mother's incapacity. Attempts at identification with the mother were interpreted. She lay in bed all day "like a corpse," and was upset over flowers placed in her hospital room. She was told to bring two pictures of her mother to the therapeutic sessions for demarcation exercises and did so in the fifth session but refused to view them until three more hours had been concluded. When she did look at one of them she screamed, "That's her!" and began to cry. She refused to face the picture while she cried, since "Mother never cried, not even when Daddy died." She then told in some detail the circumstances of her mother's last two days of life and her death. After three sessions of demarcation exercises, Julia recalled the final day of her mother's life with appropriate and genuine feelings. She also talked more openly than before of the abusive treatment she had suffered and was able to verbalize wishing from time to time that her mother were dead.

At this point Julia's dreams about her mother were primarily concerned with running away and attempting to escape the powerful, vindictive parent. Ward nurses reported that she had put aside her cheerful facade and become more overtly depressed and withdrawn. When her linking object, the robe, was brought to therapy in a paper bag she postponed touching it, finally doing so with panic and screams of, "Let me out of here! I can't stand it!" During later sessions in which she was asked to examine the robe, to describe it, and to verbalize all of the feelings it evoked, she was flooded with emotions of anger and sadness and wept, giving more details about the day of her mother's death, particularly details connected with her linking object.

Again her dreams altered. Now her mother was shrunken, small, and powerless. In one dream she floated in a tiny casket. Julia's nurses observed her "getting worse," and on the ward she seemed anxious and agitated. Therapy then focused on the funeral. Julia discussed it in detail and recalled the minister's sermon, having further emotional storms as she did so. She confessed how she had wanted praise at the funeral and how she had hoped that protracted mourning would inspire praise and sympathy. The minister had praised her masochistic devotion and wished her luck and happiness in her new freedom. These remarks evoked intense feelings of guilt.

In subsequent sessions she described the funeral at greater length and reported dreaming of a cemetery in which mourners, her mother among them, looked disappointed at the absence of a grave. In another dream her mother appeared in a wheelchair, and Julia pushed her off a cliff, noticing that the old woman did not seem to object.

By the time Julia had had twenty sessions, she made her first attempts at directing psychic investment toward new objects. She spoke of the possibility of resuming the relationship she had enjoyed with a former suitor. Now she was able to view, without apparent anxiety, her mother's picture and the photograph of her mother's grave that we had asked a relative to provide. The photographs and the robe, which had been kept until that time, were returned to her, and she and the therapist looked at advertisements for tombstones in the therapist's office. Although she had arranged for a marker for her father's grave within a month of his death, she had not been able after eight months to order her mother's. She could now talk much more realistically than before about the death and was no longer intensely occupied with thoughts about her mother. She began to leave the hospital for weekends out of town, and reported enjoying herself for "the first time" in her life. Two sessions later she announced that she had burned the red robe and ordered a tombstone. She also spoke of a dream that reflected the rage that lay within her mourning; in it the therapist appeared with a ring through his nose and another in his ear—she was now making a monkey out of her physician. Her transferred anger was then interpreted.

The final step in her re-griefing was a visit to the grave. She had been afraid to return to the cemetery since the burial and was anxious at first over the proposed visit, doubting that she would be able to go through with it. At the graveside she was encouraged by Sarvay, who assisted the senior author in Julia's treatment and accompanied her there, to associate freely and to verbalize her thoughts about the body within. She was able to talk realistically about it and seemed quite relaxed within a few minutes. Therapy was then terminated. A three-year follow-up by

mail showed that she was doing well; her established pathological grief symptoms did not return.

Since Julia was under study in a pilot research project
on re-grief therapy, she had been given, among other tests
that will not be referred to in this paper, the MMPI on three
occasions: at the beginning of re-grief therapy; in mid-

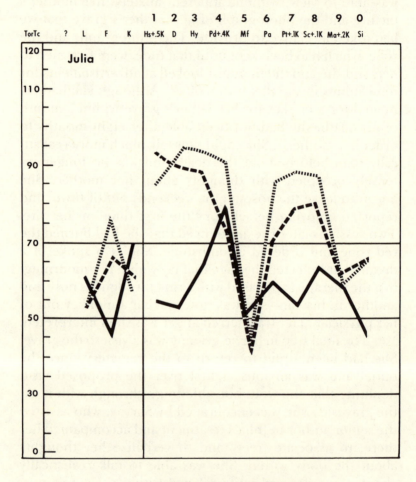

---- First MMPI profile (July 10)
..... Second MMPI profile (July 23)
___ Last MMPI profile (August 14)

course, when it was predicted that she would have emotional storms; and at the conclusion of our work with her. To determine whether the magnitude of change in the scores from one testing to another was clinically significant, we used a procedure recommended by Schofield (1966). The degree of T-score change necessary for clinical "significance" was 14 points for scale 2; 12 points for scale 6; 10 points for scales 3, 4 and 9; and 8 points for scales 1, 5, 7 and 8. These are based on estimations of the standard error of measurement of each scale and provide a way to measure the clinically significant change in each patient by comparison of his MMPI scores. It was to be expected that Julia's second MMPI profile would reflect the state in which she was exhibiting emotional storms and disorganization. The final test would be expected to reflect reorganization —the completion of a grieving process.

Julia's first MMPI profile showed marked elevation on scales 2, 3, 4, 1, 6, 7, and 8 in that order, with peaks at 2 (T=94) and 7 (T=88). The second profile showed a significant decrease in scale 1 and a significant increase in scales 4, 6, 7, and 8, which reflects ongoing emotional storms in the first half of re-grief therapy. Between the second and third MMPI testing there was a decrease in scales 1, 2, 3, 6, 7, and 8, as predicted. This reflects a successful resolution of the emotional storming and re-griefing process. Finally, the comparison between the first and last testing scores shows significant decrease in scales 1, 2, 3, 6, 7, and 8. The pattern is similar to that of Mike, a twenty-three-year-old man hospitalized with the classic symptoms of pathological grief, whose case is discussed in detail elsewhere (Volkan 1971). It reflects the impressive overall improvement that occurred as a result of re-grief therapy. Improvement occurs chiefly in the second half of the course of re-griefing, after linking objects have been used to stimulate and free emotions that have been frozen until then, and to bring related thought processes into play. In Mike's case the interim MMPI showed a significant increase in scale 8 and evidenced decompensation and the occasional appearance of schizophrenic-like ideation. His final MMPI profile showed little change in basic personality structure but a marked reduction of his symptoms, particu-

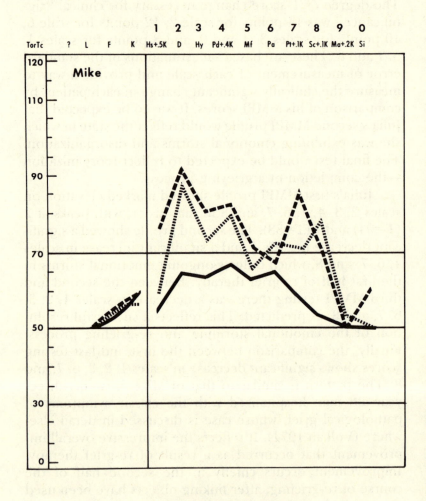

---- First MMPI profile (May 1)
..... Second MMPI profile (June 3)
___ Last MMPI profile (July 1)

larly those of depression and anxiety. A comparison of Mike's first with his final profile again suggests the successful completion of re-grief therapy inasmuch as it indicates "significant" decrease in scales 1, 2, 3, 4, 5, 7, and 8.

CHIP. Chip, a twenty-year-old student treated by Sarvay for established pathological mourning was eleven when his father began a struggle with lung cancer that lasted for two years. His death initially brought Chip relief not only from having to witness his father's agony but also from having to endure his always ready criticism, and the boy experienced no acute grief. Two weeks later, however, he became depressed and was beset by feelings of worthlessness. The symptoms of chronic depression and of established pathological grief (preoccupation with the father's image and a sense of his continuing presence) alternated and became part of his life experience. When he entered college two-and-a-half years before coming to our attention, his symptoms became more severe. His father had attended the same college, and Chip was paying his tuition from money his father had set aside for the purpose. Although Chip did well scholastically, he felt that he was failing to live up to fantasized expectations of his dead father and finally sought psychiatric help.

The initial formulation of his case pointed to an unresolved oedipal struggle. Chip was the eldest son; his younger brother had come when Chip was five and had preempted their father's attention. When Chip reached puberty, the father's long illness and his death did not permit the boy to resolve the oedipal struggle with him during a time when he might have been said to have a second chance to do so. Chip kept his dead father alive through the splitting mechanism and continued to behave as though he were still under his parent's rigid dominance.

Sarvay told Chip at the outset that his treatment would focus on the father's death in an effort to bring him relief by re-griefing him. The treatment took two months and five days, during which time Chip was seen as an outpatient for twenty-six therapeutic sessions. During the first hours Chip readily talked of his need to keep his father alive in order to "acquire his love and approval." He felt—in a reflection of his introject—"as if my father is part of me." He used the word "merge" in describing his total, albeit transient, identifications with the dead man.

His preoccupations affected his approach to girls. For six months before he came into treatment he had been steadily dating a girl who had severe bronchial asthma, recalling the father's lung disease and depression. Chip fantasized rescuing her (symbolically rescuing his father). He continued to speak in the present tense about his parent and referred to "my father's room" and "my father's house" in spite of the length of time his father had been dead.

During the final two weeks of his father's life, Chip and his brother had been sent to live with friends. He later learned that at the end his father had been "out of his head" and had asked that his oxygen be cut off. His physician allegedly complied, and within a few minutes the father was dead. Chip became enraged when describing this event, crying, "He died like a dog!" He perceived his father's decision as selfish and cowardly and felt that his father should have fought to stay alive rather than "copping out on him." At the funeral he refused to view the body and confided "I was afraid he would sit up." He saw only a glimpse of the coffin as it was carried from the church and felt that perhaps his father was not inside. At the first therapeutic session he reported a dream that illustrated the conflict between his desire to kill his father and to keep him alive. In the dream his father was in the hospital, where he had been pronounced dead. The scene then changed and the dead father was coming home. Initially happy to see him, Chip then felt anger at his return. The father ignored the son and disrupted the household. Chip ran up to his parent and touched his face, which felt like soft clay and fell apart under his fingers. Chip awakened in great anxiety.

In therapy he described his father's many accomplishments at length and regarded him with awe. Yet he complained of his father's cold indifference and the violence of his disapproval. At last he said, "I think he almost said he loved me near the end but he couldn't—it would have killed him," and wept for the first time since he became a patient. The therapist then asked directly about any fantasy that Chip might have about having contributed to his father's death. He then verbalized a fantasy of having murdered his father with his feelings; he had often wished for the death in order to be free, and when his mother told him that death was expected within a month he circled on his calendar the date, which had been accurately predicted. The fact that he had done this added further weight to his fantasy.

After this disclosure Chip began giving more memories of the last days of his father, who had seemed "gray and ghostlike" and "hollow and dead inside" during this time. Since Chip had described himself in much the same terms, the identification was pointed out to him. He brought to the eighth session an envelope containing several photographs of his father, as he had been instructed. At first he exhibited very little affect when he looked at them, but then he became anxious, turning them face down and crying, "I can't look any longer. I am afraid I will see myself in the pictures and everything I am not." As the demarcation exercise went on he was asked to describe his father's features in the pictures, to describe his own, and to verbalize what they had in common and where they were different. When Chip noticed a cigarette in his father's hand he began to cry, screaming that as a child he had often taken cigarettes to his father to please him, but they had killed him. During the second session with the pictures, it was learned that Chip had a second set, pictures of his father showing the emaciation of his last year of life. Chip had avoided looking at them "because they look like pictures of a dead man." He was asked to bring them, however, along with his father's bloodstone ring, an heirloom from seven generations that had become his linking object. He kept it in a box rather than wearing it, on the grounds that the stone might break if it were worn and that this would mean the loss of his "last link" with his father.

Demarcation exercises with the first set of photographs continued, and Chip was asked to describe what was pictured and to verbalize his associations and memories. At each session he wept. He spoke of his father in health and in illness as though they were two persons. Looking at his father's youthful image he explained, "This is my father, vital, alive—everything I want to be," but when asked to touch the pictured face he refused, saying he was afraid of blocking out his father's face. This fear was interpreted as fear of killing his father again, this time with his finger. His reaction to the second set of photographs was quite different. They aroused little affect. He said, "This picture is a lie. He is just a shell, a dead man. I feel like I should cry but I can't. It is not real." Thus he demonstrated splitting of both the father, as symbolically represented, and his own ego.

For the first five weeks Chip emphasized the negative aspects of his relationship with his father, repeatedly speaking of his lack of warmth and demonstrativeness. Nonetheless evidence of warm moments with his father surfaced in these sessions. It appeared that father and son had spent considerable time together and that during the summer before his death, particularly, his father had done many things with his son. Family members told Chip how during the last two weeks of his life the dying man had spoken of his pride in his two sons and his love for them. Chip insisted on discounting and rationalizing this, saying "I wish I could believe that, but I know it's a lie." Even when he remembered his father's direct expression of affection for him he scoffed at its "phoniness." Interpretation suggested that Chip in refusing to accept the positive aspects of the relationship was trying to avoid feeling that he had killed someone who loved him. Chip then had an emotional storm, saying, "I killed him because he wasn't there when I wanted him. Now he is always around and I can't get rid of him!" The narcissistic blow of his father's death was evident in this outcry.

The dichotomy of the "dead" and "live" father was repeatedly pointed out to Chip. In order to work on the splitting, he was asked to examine a picture of the "dead" man alongside one of the "live" man and to contrast them, naming each as he did so. He called the "dead" father Daddy but used his first name, Jim, in pointing to the "live" one, experiencing an emotional storm as he did so. At the end of the hour he cried out, "They are the same person. They are both dead. Now I have nothing!" The exercises with the photographs continued over several more sessions and resulted in considerable expression of feeling and a marked increase of sadness. Chip recalled in greater detail the pain of watching his father die. He had carefully avoided telling him good-bye on his last visit, thinking magically that if he failed to say good-bye he would not die. He began recalling more and more of the warm moments with his father. For the first time in six months he dated someone other than his chronically ill girl friend; during his second month of therapy he reported going on a blind date and greatly enjoying it, but on the following day he became severely depressed. It was suggested that he was feeling guilt over having enjoyed himself—and over having let down his ill friend (father). He became more confused than before about the boundaries between himself and his father, expressing uncertainty about whether his academic grades were his own or his father's. He said he was ashamed to speak of his A average because it might be clear that the grades were not his own but his father's. In further evidence of destructive identification, he described his body as "no good" and "rotting inside." The identification was interpreted and in the eighth week, when he was encouraged to speak of the funeral, he did so with much affect.

Chip was angry as he told of being excluded from the family's grieving. He had been sent to friends and saw his mother at the funeral for the first time after he had learned of the death from her. He rode to the funeral with other children rather than with his mother and sat with them in church. Remembering the ceremony he screamed, "It was pagan—vultures from everywhere pretending how sorry they were—they just threw him in the ground!" A second MMPI was given, and this was reflected in a transference manifestation. Chip was angry at having to take the test again and directed his anger toward the therapist, describing him in terms he had used earlier for his father. Interceptive interpretation was immediately made, and Chip sadly described feeling that his father was now gone. "It hurts—I miss him. I have lost everything." The therapist had kept the bloodstone ring in his desk and when he produced it Chip cried, "That is the link! It is a legacy. I'm not worthy of it!" and refused to open the box.

Two sessions later Chip showed signs of successful reorganization and was making active efforts to establish new emotional investments. He made new friends and began to take pride in himself and his work, no longer appearing depressed. He enthusiastically made plans for the future, stopped being preoccupied with thoughts of his father, and, for the first time, accepted credit for his own accomplishments. He decided to break off his relationship with his sickly girl friend and seek girls "with more life." The father's pictures, which the therapist had been keeping in his office, were returned, and he had one framed to stand on his dresser. After doing this he spoke of having a much greater sense of personal identity. "I look at the picture and I know that it is he, my dead father; and I am me." This time when the therapist put the ring box on his desk Chip readily picked it up, slipped the ring on the little finger, as his father had worn it, and then placed it on his ring finger where he left it. "I like it better this way," he said. "After all, it is my ring."

In his next-to-last session, Chip reported a dream in which his father had been frozen, to be reanimated when a cure for his disease should be found. The father asked to

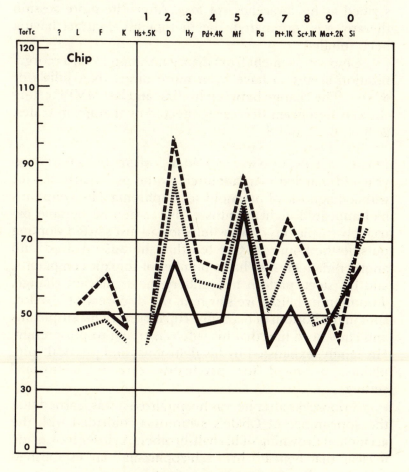

---- First MMPI profile (March 10)
..... Second MMPI profile (April 24)
___ Last MMPI profile (May 13)

be thawed out, although he knew this would mean his death. His request was honored, and he returned home for a final meal with his family. Although everyone in the family circle realized that the father was going to die, there was an atmosphere of acceptance and peace. Then the father rose and said good-bye to Chip. When Chip awakened from this dream, he had a transient feeling of sadness that he described as his awareness of loss. After one more session therapy was terminated, the therapeutic contract having been fulfilled.

Chip's movement from disorganization toward reorganization seems to have been more direct than Julia's or Mike's. The change between his first and last MMPI testing showed significant decreases effected by therapy in scales, 2, 3, 4, 6, 7, and 8.

CLYDE.   Clyde, who was treated by Volkan, was a thirty-six-year-old married man admitted to the psychiatric service with a diagnosis of paranoid schizophrenia. His symptoms had appeared eight months earlier, when he became extremely suspicious of his wife. She had just started working outside the home, and he felt that she was involved with another man. He also had a number of somatic complaints, and his sleep pattern had undergone significant change. Two months before we saw him, the discovery of a yellow spot in the bottom of his coffee cup increased his suspicions and convinced him that his wife was trying to poison him. His family, exhausted by his delusional and physical complaints, arranged for psychiatric care in a hospital setting.

Two weeks after he was hospitalized it was learned that the appearance of Clyde's symptoms coincided with the accidental drowning of his half-brother. A closer look made it clear that beneath his "schizophrenia" lay established pathological mourning.

His mother had died of melanoma after a lengthy illness when Clyde, the eldest of three children, was thirteen.

Shortly thereafter the father remarried and begat three more children. Clyde and a full sister each underwent surgery for melanoma within eleven years of their mother's death and lost an aunt to the same disease, so it was not surprising that he reacted to his half-brother's sudden death with great anxiety. Very early in his treatment we understood how his main delusion related to his complicated grief. The yellow spot in the cup represented melanoma, the sign of anxiety and death. The coffee in the cup stood for the muddy waters in which his fifteen-year-old half-brother had drowned while fishing.

News that his brother was in trouble had reached Clyde when he was home alone, putting a stack of records on his record player. It was several hours before the body of the boy was recovered, and during this interval his brother refused to believe that death had taken place; friends encouraged his hope that all would turn out well. After the body was found and identified, Clyde still could not accept the reality of what had happened.

Since the body had been so long in the water, it was necessary to arrange quickly for the burial. Clyde, the eldest man in the family since the death of his father ten years earlier, was so occupied with funeral plans that he had no time to express his grief. He later described the funeral as a tearless, unemotional affair. He left the cemetery before the body was lowered into the grave and did not return. Friends accepted the death as being God's will, but Clyde felt anger, which he suppressed, and was hypercritical of himself, saying that he had failed the youngster and that if he had accompanied him the drowning would not have occurred. Obsessed with the boy's image, he continued to speak of him frequently in the present tense.

Clyde's re-grief therapy, like Julia's, took place in a hospital setting. It lasted little more than two months. He was seen four times weekly. At the start Clyde remembered the repeating dreams he had had after the death. They involved his diving into muddy water to save his brother, searching unsuccessfully for him. He would awake with anxiety. Since the death he had been concerned with teaching his children to swim lest they drown in a shallow brook on his property. Soon the therapist learned that Clyde, after his own brush with death, wanted to make sure that he could save himself and bargained with the threat of melanoma by becoming a "good" person—one who did not express anger and who did not question God's will as manifested in the drowning.

Encouraged by the therapist, he talked about his brother during the early sessions. He insisted that he had failed his brother and expressed strong feelings of guilt about the accident. In his attempt to keep his brother alive he signed up to study electronics, with the idea of finishing a television set his brother had been putting together. Again, severe headaches led him to abandon this course.

Early in treatment the therapist tried to learn why Clyde's paranoid ideation was so greatly concerned with his wife. It came out that the brother had called Clyde's home asking for a loan on the day before he died. Clyde's wife had talked to him and refused the money, which was wanted for the purchase of a car; the couple had previously discussed the boy's reckless driving. Displacement accounted for Clyde's anger, since he saw her as failing the boy just before he died. An interesting feature of the relationship between husband and wife was his high degree of dependency on her and his sensitivity to separation from her. The family history of melanoma had led to a realistic sense of caution, exemplified by his protecting his skin from sunlight. When his brother died, Clyde's anxiety about his own death was exacerbated, and the idea of separation from his wife required solution. His delusional system was, in a sense, in the service of pushing his wife into a divorce; he was forestalling the dereliction of the woman he depended on by paradoxically initiating separation on his own terms. These two interpretations of what was going on between man and wife were adhered to by the therapist throughout Clyde's griefwork and offered for his consideration each time he reintroduced his delusional system about her faithlessness.

Clyde brought his brother's picture to the fourth session. The therapist took it from its envelope and placed it face down before his patient. This practice, customary in re-griefing, grants the patient the initiative of looking at the picture when he is ready. Clyde made no immediate move to examine it. During this interview he reported an incident that helped him toward insight. On the previous day he had spilled coffee on his neck and shirt collar while talking to a medical student on the ward and had jokingly but anxiously remarked that he was trying to drown himself. The therapist complimented him on the astuteness of his observation and suggested that he felt the same way about his unexpressed emotions concerning his brother's death, fearing that their expression would end up by drowning him. From this point on, Clyde showed an increasing ability to express his angry feelings, and by the end of the hour he stated that his brother had been a fat show-off who had been stupid in getting himself drowned and making all kinds of complications.

While telling about a dream that occurred at the end of the first week of re-griefing, Clyde had his first intense emotional storm. In it Clyde had seen his eldest son and the thought "kill! kill!" came to him. He spontaneously associated the dead brother with his son, and in so doing consciously acknowledged his feelings of aggression toward his brother. Toward the end of the hour he related another dream he had had shortly after agreeing to start re-grief therapy. In this he had been in a dark valley, riding a bicycle. He rode on a wet and slippery road but was able to hurry along and escape an impending storm. At the end of this session the therapist complimented him on his tolerance of the emotional discharge that had taken place. He warned him that the process was not yet over but encouraged him by saying that the experience of similar feelings might not be so frightening in future.

The next day there was another dream. Clyde had seen a small man and a tall, dark one whose shoes were old and comfortable, with wrinkles. Clyde's association to the dream indicated that he was the little man, who had felt humble all his life and who had tried not to provoke trouble such as the melanoma sent by God's will. The tall man represented the therapist. His shoes indicated wide travel, and they had an easy fit. Clyde's shoes were uncomfortable, and they fit poorly; he longed for more comfortable ones. After reporting this dream, Clyde began to tell about his first delusion after the drowning. This had led him to believe that the soles of his feet were red and itching because of a powder his wife had put in his socks to poison him. Although he had not seen his brother's feet after he drowned, he had seen his hands, wrinkled because of long immersion. After talking about his foot delusion, he made his first attempt to look at the photograph but could not. He felt cold. The interpretation of this was that his brother was cold in death. He sighed and declared emotionally, "I wish I could start living again!" The wish to keep in contact with the dead brother through internalization of him was interpreted. He was reminded of his earlier dream of "kill! kill!" and had another emotional experience.

During the next session he looked for the first time at the picture and exclaimed, "He's dead and I had nothing to do with it!" He began to cry and talked about how handsome his brother looked and how sad it was that he had died on the threshold of manhood. About this time Clyde's behavior on the ward changed considerably. He gave up reporting his delusional ideas to ward personnel and other patients. He went into what he called a state of grieving, weeping violently and suddenly becoming angry with the dead boy. In this agitated state he shouted at the introject within his breast several times, saying in the same words Mike (Volkan 1971) used in screaming at the introject of his father, "Leave me alone! Get out! Get out!" On the following day Clyde commented to his therapist that he felt better than at any time during the year just past.

At this point, after a month of therapy, he was asked to direct his attention to the receipt of the tragic news and the funeral. He reported a dream in which he was relaxing comfortably in what might have been his own home. After a knock on the door, a tall woman appeared. He explained to her that he was "just relaxing—waiting for my brother." The tall woman was associated with a next-door neighbor whose house his children frequented. Finding himself alone at home since his brother's drowning, he had felt uneasy, rejected, and emotionally separated from his wife and the children who so often played next door. When this association was worked out he was able to laugh and to say, "Here I go again—sour grapes. Yes, I was very mad at my kids, who left me alone by going to the neighbor's house."

The records he was about to listen to when the news of the death came had become his linking object. They were brought to the hospital, and the patient and his therapist listened to them—the same ones he had not been able to bring himself to listen to or to touch since his brother's death. The experience brought on a flood of emotions, and Clyde cried aloud for a long time. The next day he exhibited abortive emotional spells, saying "ah-ah," but being unable to continue. He finally described a "weight on his chest" that he wanted to remove. Then he voluntarily suggested that he and the therapist talk about "that fellow"— the dead brother. He recalled how reckless the dead boy had been and how unrealistically he had dreamed of the future. He kept asking his therapist, "What do you do with a fellow like that? How do you advise him?" as though his brother were still alive and the questions still awaited solution. At the height of this negative outburst, the therapist asked, "He was a big show-off, wasn't he?" to which Clyde replied by expressing anger and explaining that it was his brother's recklessness that had led them to withhold money and that had, in the end, killed him.

Clyde then told of something that had angered him at his brother's funeral. The boy's friends had come from a distance for the funeral and spoke of seeing the town as soon as the services were over. They rationalized this proposal by saying that the dead boy had so often spoken of a certain part of town that he had awakened their interest in seeing it for themselves. Clyde felt that these mourners were behaving like casual tourists and that he was pressed into service as a tour guide even before the coffin was finally put in the ground. The therapist then asked him how he knew that his brother had actually been buried and reminded him that he was so much preoccupied with his brother's image that he had in effect buried him in his own breast rather than in a grave.

The therapist asked Clyde to get snapshots of the grave for use at the therapeutic sessions. This created a sudden interest in various aspects of the burial—the depth of the grave, the efficacy of the concrete vault, the absence of a marker—all the preoccupations typical of pathological mourning and indicative of anxiety that the dead might rise. Toward the end of the second month Clyde reported a dream in which he had found himself alone at the grave and had lowered the casket containing his brother's body into the vault and fastened the cover. He had started shoveling dirt into the grave when a second man—probably the therapist—appeared and joined him in this work.

During this time Clyde began trying to reinvest in new objects the attachments withdrawn from the dead brother in the course of re-griefing. He was concerned about improving the relationship with his wife, returning to work, and assuming normal involvements and activities. A sportsman most of his life, he had given up sports after the drowning, but once again he expressed an interest in golf, fishing, and hunting. He reported feeling more relaxed and his behavior during the interviews bore this out. He voluntarily brought a cup of coffee to one interview and drank it before the therapist.

Next day, in spite of considerable anxiety, he went to a funeral home and asked about monuments. At the end of two months of hospitalization he spent a weekend at home with his family and twice visited his half-brother's grave, which he had avoided since the funeral. He also visited his stepmother and with her decided on a marker to be put on the grave. A few days later he was discharged from the hospital and his re-grief therapy was at an end. He was seen for follow-up three times during the first post-treatment year, twice during the second year, and once during the third. At the fifth follow-up interview, a year and nine months after termination, Clyde reported what we felt was a "review dream." In it he was swimming with his ten-year-old son, who wrestled with him. Clyde disengaged himself by swimming away, but the son turned into someone large and dark who recommenced the struggle in the water. Although anxious, Clyde felt confident enough in his superior swimming ability to separate himself and swim to safety. Clyde's associations to this indicated that during his re-griefing he had associated his son with the lost brother, but that he now enjoyed a better relationship with the boy. The drowned brother had in a sense tried to draw Clyde under the water, but Clyde could now save himself and differentiate himself from the one who drowned. Nevertheless, he wondered whether he had left the door open to the denial of the drowning and was puzzled by his inability to recall its exact date. After this interview he went to the county offices for a copy of the death certificate.

He talked about the past anniversary of his brother's death and felt some anxiety which he connected with that date. With this insight he decided to visit the graveside rather than continue feeling anxious, and the visit did allay his anxiety. He was now able to use his linking objects simply as records to be played, and he resumed golf and hunting, diversions he had given up during his pathological period because of their "aggressive nature." He was no longer phobic about guns or hunting.

Clyde seemed to have accomplished a great deal by himself, although he was still rather markedly cautious. When he reviewed his erstwhile symptoms, he stated, surprisingly, that one of the reasons his brother's death had so strongly affected him was that he had become sensitized toward loss at the age of twelve when his mother died. At the time of this interview many of his fellow-workers were being laid off and his job also was in jeopardy, but he seemed able to handle this threat in a reality-oriented way. By his final interview during his third post-therapy year he still had his job and was carrying on in his normal life-style without further preoccupation with his brother's image.

Despite his presenting symptoms (circumscribed paranoid ideation and numerous somatic complaints), Clyde had a fairly flat pretherapy MMPI profile. There were peaks at scales 8, 6, and 2; however, only 8 was above $T=70$. The validity scales were within normal limits for Clyde as they were for the other patients reported on almost every testing. As his therapist anticipated, scales 1, 2, and 4 increased significantly in the second MMPI testing. Patients often seem worse midway through their therapeutic course as they are picked up in the throes of the re-griefing process. There was significant decrease in scales 1, 2, 3, 4, and 7 between the second and third use of the MMPI. However, only one scale changed significantly between the first and final testing; this was scale 8. Other scales decreased slightly, below the level of significance. This may reflect the limited initial elevation on the MMPI scales displayed by Clyde in all but scale 8. The significant increase in "psychopathology" halfway through Clyde's re-griefing and a

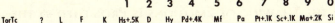

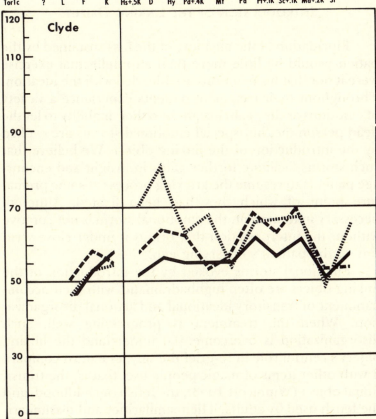

---- First MMPI profile (January 26)
..... Second MMPI profile (February 16)
___ Last MMPI profile (March 3)

corresponding decrease with the termination of therapy, as predicted, are striking. The fact that Clyde showed significant improvement only on scale 8 remains to be accounted for. It is certainly possible that the second MMPI testing gave a more accurate indication of the extent of pathological mourning as it appeared in the first stages of re-griefing.

WHY THE THAWING OF EMOTIONS IS PROMOTED BY THE INTRODUCTION OF THE LINKING OBJECT

Elucidation of the meaning of the loss sustained by the patient would be little more than an intellectual exercise were it not that his emotions are blended with the ideation. Throughout their treatment patients experience a variety of emotions as they gain insight into their inability to let the dead person die, but special emotional storms are evoked by the introduction of the linking object. We believe that such storms facilitate further gains in insight and encourage patients to resume the grieving process at some premature point of which they had been fixated. Although necessary in treatment, the emotional storm is not curative without the interpretation that brings it under close scrutiny of the patient's observing ego.

Emotional storms evoked by the introduction of the linking object are often highly dramatic, with their accompaniment of transitory ideational and actional disorganization. When the treatment is progressing well, such disorganization is overcome. To understand the linking object's central role in re-grief therapy, one must compare it with other items of magic people use; that is, the transitional object (Winnicott 1953), the fetish of childhood, and the fetish used by adults. Their similarities and dissimilarities have been explored in an article by the senior author (1972b). In order to show how the linking object contains congealed emotions, especially those clearly related to aggression, it will be necessary to consider here only certain of its aspects.

The transitional object, of which Linus's blanket is a popularly known example, is an object that "becomes vitally important to the child . . . more important than the mother, an almost inseparable part of the child" (Winnicott 1953). Chosen on the basis of texture, odor, visibility, and movability from whatever is available to the infant in the first year of life, it is the first "not-me"—but not altogether "not-me." It links "not-me" with "mother-me" (Greenacre 1969; 1970). It absorbs neglect and abuse as well as the most loving closeness. It is a consolation for separation, as in going to sleep. The anxiety of some children over psychic separation from the mother is, however, so intense that they use their comforting objects in bizarre ways that cause us to speak of the childhood fetish. We see the transitional object, as well as the childhood fetish that originates in the transitional object, on a spectrum that ranges from normalcy at one end to pathology on the other. Recent work on the transitional object (Fintzy 1971; Greenacre 1969, 1970; Modell 1970; Volkan 1973) shows it as a Janus-like facilitator of the acceptance of reality on the progressive side and of the denial of reality on the regressive side. One might envision a lantern with one opaque and one transparent side; when the transparent side is turned out the outside world is illuminated, but when the other side is turned out the world slips into darkness and is lost. As time goes on the magic of the original transitional object is slowly diminished; Winnicott (1953) suggested that its memory is not subject to repression, and that it may reappear in later life when deprivation threatens the individual. In the life of the person with borderline personality organization it may continue to exist in covert fashion (Fintzy 1971; Volkan 1973), fostering the illusion in such a person that since the transitional object is under his absolute control, the environment is also under his dominion. In such an illusion the individual exercises the privilege of acknowledging or disavowing the existence of any external object according to the pressure of his anxieties and wishes; thus he can see the world as he wants it to be rather than as it is.

Are linking objects reactivated transitional objects? Certainly the illusion of control over them gives the patient the illusion that he can kill the dead or retain a link with him (bring him to life). The senior author (1972*b*) raised the question as to whether those suffering from established pathological mourning had been unusually attached as children to transitional objects or childhood fetishes. Although re-griefing yields little genetic history as compared with the genetic reconstructions in a transference neurosis, the psychoanalysis or intensive psychoanalytically oriented psychotherapy undergone by ten of our patients with established pathological mourning disclosed sensitization to separation in early childhood. For example, Mike's mother had had manic-depressive episodes that required occasional hospitalization when he was very young (Volkan 1971).

Although no transitional object was reactivated in its childhood form, the dynamic processes that through it had fostered the child's illusory power of control over the environment were. Separation problems at the transitional object level are, to be sure, condensed in the linking object, but to them have been added the answers to separation occurring on higher developmental levels as well. Each makes it possible not to acknowledge a loss and thus to exclude it from experience. In certain specifics, the magic of each is similar. Like the child who refuses fully to accept his newly laundered security blanket until it begins to feel and smell as it did before, one of our patients, whose linking object was the flag that had covered her soldier father's casket years earlier, went into a rage at receiving it after her mother had had it cleaned and thus altered its remembered smell and texture. A few months later this patient visited her father's grave, although since the funeral she had denied its existence. In the cemetery she found a small flag on his grave and took it away with her exclaiming with some anxiety and excitement during her next therapy hour, "Now I have my own flag!"

Another magical object, the adult fetish, needs consideration. In the classical sense it represents the illusory penis of the mother and may represent the last moment in which women could be regarded as phallic. We now know that it is a compromise between separation and castration (Bak 1953), but its main function is to deal with castration anxiety. If the fetishist is to be fully potent, he must have his fetish close at hand. Winnicott (1953) related it to the transitional object when he wrote, "Fetish can be described in terms of a persistence of a specific object or type of object dating from infantile experience in the transitional field, linked with the delusion of a maternal phallus." Greenacre (1970) indicated that the fetish contains congealed anger born of castration anxiety. The senior author (1972 *b*) compares the adult fetish and the linking object, concluding that unlike the former or the transitional object, the linking object has to be distanced and avoided. He suggested that like the fetish, but more significantly, it contains anger and is similarly an instrument for the control of the expression of anger that arises primarily from separation panic.

In summary we can say that as a reactivated variation of the transitional object the linking object provides an external locus in which the patient can achieve an illusion of the possibility of reunion with the dead and at the same time the possibility of killing him. The mourner defends himself against the tension generated by his ambivalent wishes by distancing his linking object. It is chiefly its ambivalent aspect that the patient faces when ready to look at his linking object during his re-griefing. The link strained with ambivalence is brought into the realm of his inner experience, and thus it is no longer possible to externalize the painful work of mourning. The result is an emotional storm. When the patient uses his linking object in therapy it is usual for his anger toward the dead to surface, a narcissistic anger, chiefly over being deserted. It had until now been congealed within the linking object; now it could come into the open.

We have noted that although the linking object has magical powers for the patient, it should provide no magical shortcut for the therapist, who must employ in his introduction of this symbol the highest awareness of unconscious psychological processes. It is his training in understanding the psychodynamic processes we have been describing, his ability to interpret and to intervene, that enable him to unfreeze the previously frozen processes of grieving by the use of the linking object. We should certainly object strongly to any view of the linking object as a mechanical aid in the treatment of established pathological mourning.

chapter 11

EXPANDING AWARENESS THROUGH SELF-CONFRONTATION METHODS

Daniel I. Malamud, Ph.D.

In the course of developing an experiential workshop in self-understanding at New York University's School of Continuing Education, I have created a large repertoire of self-confrontation exercises. These are structured activities in which I encourage members to involve themselves with an attitudinal blend of playfulness and curiosity. In designing such activities, I aim for experiences so novel that students' customary responses will be circumvented and they will have an opportunity to confront themselves from a surprising perspective. A summary of the God exercise, more fully reported elsewhere, may serve as an example:

Each member in turn creates a four act mini-play and plays all the parts. The first act consists of a dialogue between two of the student's conflicting selves, for example, between his good self and his bad self. The dialogue consists of two brief statements, first a statement by one self and then a response by the other. In the second act, the student's "parents," who were silently listening in during the first act, now each in turn make a single one-sentence statement to either of the student's two selves. The third act begins where the second act leaves off and consists of a single exchange of one sentence statements between the two "parents." In the final act, the student role-plays God, who has witnessed all three acts and addresses a statement to any of the four characters. [Malamud 1973*b*.]

As my conviction grew that effective learning about the self requires active participation and emotional involvement, I began to explore the selective application of such self-confrontation procedures with patients in individual therapy, moving beyond the usual patterns of verbal exchange and inviting them to participate during the session in one or another simple but challenging task, "game," or "experiment." My evolution as a therapist in this direction was deeply reinforced and influenced by my personal experiences with Perls and his Gestalt therapy methods (Perls 1969) and by Assagioli's (1965) writings on psychosynthesis.

In a previous paper (1973*a*) I presented a series of brief vignettes from my work with different patients illustrating my use of the tape recorder, my introduction of predesigned projective exercises, and how I capitalize on spontaneous events in the session to create a relevant exercise or "game" on the spot. Below I present a detailed example of my way of using self-confrontation methods, this time in the form of an abbreviated transcript of a session with Martha, a woman in her early thirties, who had been in treatment with me for about a year. Perfectionistic, overly concerned about performing well, Martha was an emotionally inhibited person who had renounced her spontaneous inner child in favor of whatever safety she could derive from being "good," hard-working, and self-controlled. The session began with a two-minute silence.

MARTHA: I can't think of anything important to say.

DR. M. (*Playfully*): Can you think of something *unimportant* to say? Something just as unimportant as can be?

MARTHA: I felt rushed coming over here, and I still feel rushed.

DR. M. (*With a somewhat ironic smile*):   That's unimportant?

MARTHA (*In utter seriousness*):   Yes. That's not important at all.

DR. M.:   Would you put those two sentences together, please. Say, "I still feel rushed, and that's unimportant."

MARTHA (*Said without affect, like a dutiful student*):   I still feel rushed, and that's unimportant.

DR. M.:   Let's see how many other things you can think of to say that are unimportant. Make a list of such statements, and after each statement add, "And that's unimportant."

MARTHA (*With increased animation*):   I've been talking to a million people. And that's unimportant. I'm having a hard time in getting in the frame of mind here. And that's unimportant. And I feel at loose ends still and terribly pressured. And that's unimportant.

DR. M.:   And now, just as a change of pace, can you think of something important, and say that? Let's see what comes out.

MARTHA: It's important that I'm so disorganized. I should be more organized and more thinking about what I am going to say, and, after all, I only have a few minutes here every week so I should have thought out what I wanted to talk about.

DR. M.:   Keep talking in the same vein adding, "And that's important," after each sentence. For example, "I'm disorganized. And that's important!"

MARTHA (*With a mixture of amusement and definite conviction*):   I haven't really thought out what I should do. And that's important! I haven't gotten myself put together. And that's important! I haven't prepared myself. And that's important!

DR. M.:   Fine! Now, how about a series of statements which are neither important nor unimportant. Add after each statement, "And that's neither important nor unimportant." Let's see what comes out this time.

MARTHA: I don't know. I don't think like that. I mean, everything is either important or it is not important. There are sheep, and there are goats. I was going to say, "I have a great deal to do today," and I don't know if I want to say that is important or that it is not important. It's hard for me to think that way.

DR. M.: Let's try an experiment. From now on as you talk, after every sentence, say, "That's important," or "That's unimportant," or "That's neither important nor unimportant." OK?

MARTHA: OK. I have a new coat. That is neither important nor unimportant. I have a great many appointments this afternoon. That's important. I have a great many things I haven't done. That's important. I have things to do that I want to do. That's unimportant. I'd like to be taking a vacation. That's neither important nor unimportant. Right?

DR. M.: Are you asking me whether a vacation is important or not?

MARTHA: No. I meant I finished that. (*With the air of a good student who did what teacher asked her to*) I did that exercise.

DR. M.: And was doing that exercise important, or unimportant, or neither?

MARTHA (*Mildly irritated*): I'd like to think that everything that I do here is important, but doing that didn't feel important. So why did we do that?

DR. M.: Well, why did you go through it?

MARTHA: Because you told me to.

DR. M.: Is that important, unimportant, or neither?

MARTHA: That's important.

DR. M.: What's important?

MARTHA: Doing what you tell me to do.

DR. M.: How is that important?

MARTHA: I guess that's my central thing in life, trying to do what everybody tells me to do. And trying to manipulate it so I look good to everybody and then occasionally getting to do what it is that *I* want to do.

DR. M.: And is what you want to do important, or unimportant, or neither?

MARTHA: Not as important compared to—it sounds funny to say because you'd think what you want to do is the most important thing—but it's easier for me to bear my not doing what I want to do rather than incurring somebody else's displeasure. My whole job is seeing to it that people don't get angry. That's my whole life! And no matter what I do or say I always feel like I'm wrong.

DR. M.: And is your always feeling wrong important, unimportant, or neither?

MARTHA: I guess that's important because that's the way I feel all the time. I never feel right. Like I was thinking about quitting my job that I'm more and more sick of and going to school, and I felt very good while I was getting all those school catalogues and very much that it was right, and then suddenly I said to myself, "Oh, Martha, what's the matter with you? You have a steady job, and here you are running off after something you don't even know you want, and you'll spend all this money on tuition, and you'll spend all this time, and really if you stayed on your job and worked hard, you could make your job into something that you wanted your job to be." And so I never can keep my good feelings.

DR. M.: So did you talk back to Critical Martha?

MARTHA: No. I just felt terrible for the rest of the day.

DR. M.: How about talking back to her now. (*Martha had permitted me to tape our sessions. My tape recorder has a remote control microphone that enables me to play back any portion of the tape and to repeat such playbacks as often as I wish. I now play back Critical Martha's statement, "Oh, Martha, what's the matter with you?" etc. several times while Martha listens intently.*) OK. Now what do you feel like saying back to her?

MARTHA (*As Criticized Martha talking back to Critical Martha*):   So what does it hurt to send away for a few catalogues? If I really want to do that, and if I really want to sit there and read them, and if it makes me feel good, then that's good enough reason to do it. I haven't signed up for anything. I haven't done anything. I just read a few catalogues, and I enjoyed doing it. I haven't hurt you one little bit. I haven't gone off and left my responsibilities or my duties, or anything.

DR. M.:   And Critical Martha answers?

MARTHA (*As Critical Martha*):   You're dreaming! You're wasting time and money! You dream all these dreams, and you think about doing this or that, and you get yourself all excited about something that just isn't realistic. Now you've got a good job, and you ought to work at it. What do you know about anything else? You spent fifteen years learning your job, and so now you want to throw all of that away.

(*As Criticized Martha*)   Oh, for God's sake! Just leave me alone! For once, let me just do something that makes me feel good. It doesn't make me feel good going to that job. It doesn't make me feel good, and I've heard about my responsibilities, and I've done my responsibilities all my life, and now I just want to have a good time.

DR. M.:   Say that last sentence again.

MARTHA (*With more emphasis*):   I've heard about responsibility, and I've done responsibility my whole entire life, and I just want to have a good time. No matter if it is foolish. I just want to do something that makes me feel happy. Before it's too late! I've been good, good, good, and I'm not doing anything I want to do.

DR. M.:   And your critic replies?

MARTHA: You'll be sorry. You know yourself. You'll do it for so long, you'll do it while you feel good, and then you're going to get scared. You always do. You get scared, just like when you were going over to those people for dinner.

DR. M.:   And what does Criticized Martha feel like saying back to Martha the Critic?

MARTHA (*In a quavery tone of voice*):   I get so tired of you. You just wear me down. I just want a very simple thing. I just want to do whatever it is that seems to make me feel good.

DR. M.:   Listen to yourself here. How do you sound? (*We replay her last statement several times.*)

MARTHA: I sound as if I'm pleading.

DR. M.:   Could you try it again and stand up for yourself with more vigor?

MARTHA (*As Criticized Martha*):   Just leave me alone! I've got the right to do whatever it is that makes me feel good. And I can't see that all these horrendous things will happen just because I do something that I want to do. And even if they did, even if I get halfway through school catalogues and never do anything about it, what difference does it make? I deserve one time in my life not to finish a job. It's not going to be completely my whole character falling to pieces. And it's not that important. The important thing is that I do what I want to do!

DR. M.:   Say that last sentence again.

MARTHA (*With increasing forcefulness and indignation*): The important thing is that I should do what I want to do. Everybody has the right to do some of the things they want to do. And with you it's just nag, and nag, and nag, or, "You shouldn't do this, you shouldn't do that." Everything has to be your way. You keep telling me about my being selfish. What about you? It's your way that's always right. I have to do this, I have to do that. My God, there's not a moment in the day that you're not telling me what's best for me to do. You think about something else, and let me be myself!

DR. M.:   And Critical Martha answers?

MARTHA: I'm the one who's given things up for you. I'm the one that stands for the virtues. I have responsibilities. I am hard work. You are the infantile things. You eat too much. You play too much. You just want to do what you want to do. You're doing all the things you want to do, and that's not good.

DR. M.:   Now answer her as vigorously as you can.

MARTHA (*With impressive strength*):   Well, you do have all the virtues. And there is nothing more miserable than all the virtues. You just spend all your time harping about responsibility, about what will other people think, and what's the nice thing to do, and what's the good thing to do, and what's the proper thing to do. You never think about what's the happy thing to do. There's no joy around you, for God's sake! I get one happy idea, and then you think about having a car accident!

DR. M.:   Could you quickly shift gears now? Would you sit here, please, and pretend you are your mother and that you have been listening all this time to the dialogue between these two Marthas. Now, as mother, make a brief statement to either one of them or to both of them, whichever you choose.

MARTHA (*As her mother to Critical Martha*):   You are absolutely right! I have told her a thousand times the very things that you have told her. She is a selfish, selfish girl. I gave up my whole life for her, and now she doesn't even call me. I don't have anything, she has everything, and she gave nothing in return. Because she is totally involved with what she wants! I agree with you absolutely—100 per cent!

DR. M.:   Now again, can you quickly shift gears and, sitting in this other chair, become your father and say something to either of the two Marthas, or to both. Just let it come out.

MARTHA (*As her father talking to Criticized Martha*):   I know. It was the same thing with me. Your mother and grandmother were at me all the time from the minute I walked into the house. They complained about my not making enough money, and they said I had no character, and they called me this, and they called me that, and told me what I had to do, and I just let them talk and talk, and I used to smile and nod, and I just didn't say a thing.

DR. M.:   Now, could you be your mother again and sit in her chair? You just heard what Martha's father said to Criticized Martha. Now, playing your mother, would you make a statement to your husband in response to what he just said?

MARTHA (*As mother to father, in a powerful voice*): That's a perfect example of the kind of advice you would give to someone. You have absolutely no character whatsoever! There is no one in this world who does not realize the kind of man you are. You never said the truth a day in your life. You call up your lady friends. You didn't send any money. You have never in your life met any of your responsibilities. I am the one that has to pick up after you. I'm the one that had to raise that child. I'm the one that had to do every single thing because you danced out of here and left me to do it!

DR. M.:   Now, please be Martha's father and respond to what your wife just said to you.

MARTHA (*As father to mother, in an angry voice*):   You're God-damn right I left! Who could stand being around you? You made my life miserable from the time I married you 'til the time I left you. There was absolutely nothing that you didn't have to tell me about that I wasn't doing wrong. You told me one thing after another, and you never left me alone. You were such an unpleasant, lousy person that I couldn't put up with you at all. You're lucky I didn't kill you. You're lucky I just walked out.

DR. M.:   Now, this time would you mind standing on this chair and playing God who has been listening in to this four-way drama. As God, I'd like for you to say something to any of them, or to all of them. It's up to you. Make a statement as God.

MARTHA (*As God to Criticized Martha*):   You just go out there and fight for yourself, because you are not involved in any of this. (*To Father*) And you, yes, you were irresponsible, and it would have been nice if you stuck around a little bit more. I can understand that you didn't want to put up with her, but you still have a strike against you because you should have stayed and taken care of your responsibilities. (*To Mother*) But you're absolutely terrible. You didn't do a single, solitary constructive thing with all of your "virtues." We're going to have to punish you terribly. You will have to spend time in purgatory because you aren't terribly good. Who let you out? (*She bursts into laughter, a laughter seemingly full of release and relief.*)

DR. M.:   Now will you please step out of all the role playing and just be yourself. And would you tune in to what you are feeling right now?

MARTHA: I really don't understand it, but that was fun. (*Laughs*) I never really heard anything like that!

DR. M.:   Like what, Martha?

MARTHA: Well, I never heard my father argue with my mother. I heard my mother say a lot of this. When I played my father I got from what my Aunt Kay used to say about my father, how he would just sit there, and everything was fine, great. (*As she talks her smile fades, and she begins to look gloomy.*)

DR. M.:   What's happening right now? You seem to be frowning.

MARTHA: I'm ruining it for myself. Because when I finished the play I thought it was just fun to have done it, and now I feel like pointing out to you that I made it all up, that they really didn't say that, that my mother wasn't really that bad, and my father wasn't that bad, and so that ruined it for me.

Dr. M.:   And is ruining it for yourself important or unimportant, or neither?

Martha: Well, I guess that's important.

Dr. M.:   What's important about that?

Martha: Because I never can accept any good feeling. I have to think to myself, "Martha, you were not fair. You were unkind to them, and you let Dr. M. think that they were bad, and really you made it up." And why do I feel like crying now? I don't know.

Dr. M.:   Stay with that crying feeling, please.

Martha: I guess because I punished me again. Because that's really what I did. I took away the good feeling, and I said I was bad because I maligned my parents.

Dr. M.:   Your Critical Martha put you down again. Do you want to face her and stand up for yourself?

Martha (*To Critical Martha*):   You made me cry again. Not for two seconds could I have a good time! No sirree, right away, I was wrong! You just couldn't wait to get to it. Why was I wrong? Because I maligned my mother and my father? But nobody said, "I want you to do a dialogue of something you actually heard your father and your mother say." Nobody said that. And so I had a good time doing it. But immediately, what do you do? You're on my back again. I've been wrong again! (*To Dr. M.*) I feel better now.

Dr. M.:   You've taken back some of your power from her.

Martha: That's right. But I am usually so unable to do it. You would think I wanted to do what I wanted to do, and you would think that I could do it, that I could get her not to do that. But I really have a terrible time doing it.

Dr. M.:   Doing what?

Martha: Doing what I want to do.

Dr. M.:   And is that important or unimportant, or neither important nor unimportant?

Martha: That's important! Because I certainly have

been unhappy doing what I have been doing. I've been doing what she says, and I've been absolutely miserable. I guess I've always felt if I was really good enough, then she would let me alone, and I could have time to do what I wanted to do. Then she would let me. I mean *I* would let me.

DR. M.:   We have to stop in a few minutes. How about reviewing this session by listening to the tape. You've expressed a lot today. See what reactions you have to rehearing yourself. (*I often find it useful to devote the last five minutes of a session to a review of what has happened by returning the recorder to the beginning point and then selecting at random fifteen to thirty second excerpts which sample different portions of the session. Patients are often surprised at how much they have said that is meaningful and get an overall sense of movement in the session which they might have otherwise missed.*)

MARTHA: As I listened I realized how much I've always believed that if I could be organized enough, if I could get everything on schedule, then I would have the time to do the things that I want to do. (*With vehemence*) But I never have! It doesn't work, and I guess it's never going to work. I have to realize this. And that's important! But this is very new, very hard for me to feel, because everyone I talk to really, except you, believes that it's right to be that way, to always be responsible, and to always do the right thing.

COMMENTARY

In this session I see myself as primarily a catalytic agent who introduced various tasks and "experiments" that enabled Martha to express and confront her inner critic in vivid, alive ways. As the session progressed, she sharpened her awareness of how she put herself down and kept herself feeling helpless in the face of her self-attacks, how one side of her was like her image of her mother, and how another side behaved like a frightened child. In responding to my encouragement to talk back to Critical Martha, she took an important step toward demonstrating to herself that she did have the hitherto only dimly felt strength to stand up for herself.

I recognized Martha's opening statement, "I can't think of anything important to say," as a condensed expression of some of her central dynamics, and my playful, somewhat teasing request to think of something unimportant to say was an attempt at involving her cognitively and emotionally in the implications of this sentence. After a while she began to recognize the playful spirit with which I kept repeating the question, "Is it important, unimportant, or neither?" and she responded with increasing appreciation that this "game" of mine was an attempt at focusing on a significant issue in her life.

By introducing the God exercise I presented Martha with an opportunity to learn how her inner conflicts could be viewed in terms of her relationships to each of her parents and their relationship to each other, and how she kept herself stuck in terms of identifications and disidentifications with them. In asking her to play God, I was implicitly inviting Martha to adopt a more wise and global perspective than was characteristic for her, but her way of playing God reflected how deeply wed she was to her parents' punitive orientation. Nonetheless, I believe she experienced the seed of a realization that there existed in her the potential of a higher self that could become a wise, guiding agent in her own growth. All in all, the playlet that she produced reflected her central dynamics in microcosm—especially the impact of her parental introjects—and with such dramatic clarity that we returned to it more than once in subsequent sessions.

In closing I would like to emphasize that, as is necessary in any approach, I am alert to situations when self-confrontation methods may be contraindicated. For example, some patients are so nonpsychological and concrete in their thinking that they actively dislike making believe. Also, I am cautious about adopting an active imagination-stimulating approach with patients already living too much in an autistic world or with extremely passive patients who would respond to my activity with intensified expectations that I possess magic that I would use in their behalf if they but cooperated with my requests.

chapter 12

A JUNGIAN APPROACH TO THE
EMOTION-LADEN DREAM IMAGE

Charles W. Asher, D.Min.

Questions regarding techniques of stimulating emotion, the degree and kind of intervention by the therapist, and the degree of emotion necessary to effect significant change in the patient have been pondered by representatives of many different schools of thought. Following Jung, I would like to shift the focus to the unconscious and in particular would like to illustrate by several clinical examples the importance of understanding the meaning of dream images as a way of stimulating emotion inherent in the image. Focusing on the unconscious, I allow the specific dream image to suggest to me my therapeutic approach. I ask, "By what technique is the unconscious attempting to enter consciousness, what meaning is the vehicle of the emotion, what degree of emotion is present?"

A basic assumption, of course, underlying this emphasis on the unconscious is the recognition of the autonomy of the unconscious and the wisdom and power it contains. This, I am aware, is not everyone's experience, and I can only hint at the reality of this experience that serves as the basis for my approach.

Certainly Jung experienced the power of the unconscious. He reports that there were times when it was so overwhelming in his life that if it had not been for his day-by-day work, his regular schedule of patients, the necessity of earning a living, he would have been overwhelmed by its fascinating power. He also reported that his encounter with the unconscious was the source of his later writings. Surely his meticulous scrutiny of his own as well as his patients' unconscious expressions in their personal and archetypal dimensions provides a striking illustration of one who listened and eagerly sought wisdom from the depths. His writings and research reflect his extensive efforts to understand the meaningfulness of unconscious symbolism.

This focus on the unconscious is also the distinguishing mark of Jungian analysis. The degree of involvement with unconscious expressions varies with each individual. There are many instances where I do not work directly with the unconscious at all. Usually, however, when I am working with people who are drawing on my particular skills, the analytical process is marked by careful attention on both our parts to dream, vision, and fantasy occurring in the analysis. The patient may need to be more connected to his unconscious; or he may need, when identified with unconscious contents, to be analyzed, so to speak, "out of the unconscious." More often than not both are necessary and occur regularly in analytical work.

The process by which the ego readjusts its relationship to the unconscious often results in the experience of the importance of the unconscious as a guide in matters of the psyche. Very often the patient discovers that what he knows of himself is not all there is to be known. The otherness of the unconscious, in its objective reality, begins to speak to him. The ego begins to find a new relationship to this unknown power, a discovery no less shocking to the individual than the discovery that the planets do not rotate around us. The ego's position becomes relativized in the psyche.

This experiential discovery has another implication for my approach to our subject. In relation to my patient, I do not consider myself to be the healing agent. My task is to be aware within myself of my own woundedness and healing capacities, the patient and physician within me. I want patient-physician to be in a working relationship with each other; and by attention to my own unconscious I continuously attempt to determine their relationship. In doing so, I become free to focus on the patient's woundedness and inner healer. I assume that the unconscious has the wisdom regarding my patient's inner patient-healer relationship, and through understanding the symbolic expressions of my patient's unconscious expressions I hope to provide interpretative, analogical bridges into consciousness for this wisdom.

This concern has implications with regard to other unconscious contents. Whenever I am identified with a personal and archetypal content, I will be unable to see clearly this same content in the psyche of my patient. The unconscious guides me in the process of disidentifying from these contents, a process that often occurs in direct reaction to an analytical hour. It is not unusual for me to work on one of my own dreams in reaction to a patient hour, sometimes staying but a small step ahead in my consciousness of what is happening. This small step is important. Very often there is no healing, although the therapist may feel strong—for example, when he is enacting unconsciously an archetypal motif such as the hero, sword or pillow in hand, rescuing the hidden treasure (unreleased emotion). A mechanical repetition of this archetype often results in dull heroes and paler maidens. Only when I know how this heroic struggle is occurring within me am I free to focus on its particular expression in my patient.

The careful attention to the reality of my own unconscious frees me to focus on the unconscious symbolic expressions in my patient. This is a starting point for approaching the emotion-laden dream image.

Before turning to some clinical examples, I would like to offer some brief theoretical comments regarding a Jungian understanding of emotion. These comments do not do justice to the complexity of a theory of emotion and might more accurately be called assumptions helpful to understanding how I approach the subject of emotional flooding.

Following Jung, the unconscious, the objective psyche, is structured in the form of complexes. At the core of the complexes is the archetype in its ambivalent components. The archetype reveals itself in image and emotion simultaneously, although in any particular situation one may precede and lead to the other. The image provides the meaning, and the emotion supplies the energetic, dynamic quality.

Contrary to psychoanalytic theory, and I think based on the significance given to the unconscious in Jungian psychology, emotions are viewed as the activity of the unconscious and not of the ego. Emotions are considered autonomous. They happen to the ego. The emotion does not arise out of the ego, but out of the complex the ego identifies with or aligns itself with at any particular moment. The emotion adheres or inheres in the image, and when the ego connects with a particular image emotion is released into consciousness and is experienced by the ego.

A particular hypothetical example may serve to illustrate this more clearly: A particular image of a policeman giving me a ticket, whether it is occasioned by a dream or an experience in reality, may confront me with the issue of my relationship to authority. My reaction to this image may be one of rebellion or fear or both. I am said to have an authority complex. At the core of the complex is the archetype, the reality and necessity of law and order in life itself. Since the psyche is also structured in opposites, for every policeman there is a rebel son or fearful boy. In this case my ego may have identified with the boy. Hence I feel the emotion of fear. I may have identified with the policeman and felt my own power to enforce law and order. I may, in fact, identify with both and experience a mixture of emotion. But my understanding of what my ego is aligning itself with is crucial to my conscious experience of the emotional component of the image.

I would now like to illustrate this approach in a few clinical examples.

A young clergyman brought the following dream: "I was giving birth to rats from my anus."

The dreamer felt this a bit strange and did not like the thought. It disturbed him, but he could not make sense of the dream.

The analyst suggested generally that rats are associated with the unacceptable. They are considered carriers of disease. They move aggressively in the dark. Birth from the anus, he suggested, indicates that a power issue may be in the process of coming into consciousness.

The patient quickly replied that he knew nothing of this. The therapist suggested that it was a process going on and no doubt it would take time for such a birth to occur, especially if it were unacceptable. He suggested that the patient bear in mind the image and wait and see what happened.

Suddenly the patient's face turned visibly red. With jaws clenched tightly he began to tell how, during his last year in seminary, his sister had been involved in a car accident, suffering severe brain damage, leaving her blind and emotionally at the level of a very young child. He had stood at her hospital bed the night after the accident; her head swollen beyond recognition, and he had just shaken his head in disbelief.

The analyst asked what he now felt about this.

The young man began alternately to cry and shout, "I hate him! I hate him. God damn you, God. God damn you."

The expression of alternating grief and rage lasted some twenty minutes of the session, with the patient at one point pounding violently on the floor.

The rat had been born. What was unacceptable, his rage against God, had been given birth. Rage passed into grief. Relief began to follow. He understood Job more clearly. He also began to understand that although he could not fathom what this tragedy meant to his sister, he could begin to discover what it meant to him.

In this example, the image of the rat provided a focus for the relief of grief and rage. The analyst's intuitive grasp of the symbolism and his hints at the possible meaning provided a bridge for the emotion to be released into consciousness. (The meaning of rat and anal symbolism is subject to a wide variety of interpretation; rats have positive value in some cultures.) Without being too specific, the analyst's hints provided a path for the young man's ego to draw near to the emotion present and to allow its release.

The analyst also felt the value of the image in the midst of the violent outburst of rage expressed in screams and pounding. The image enabled the analyst to temper his own fears by providing a meaning to the otherwise surprising expressions of his mild-mannered patient. In a sense, the analyst "held" the image while the patient expressed the emotion. Later they would unite again, but on a more conscious level.

A similar release of emotion may occur when a spouse who has died or been divorced or separated from returns in the patient's dream. The loved, or hated, one is very much alive in the patient's psyche, and the simple recognition of this fact by the analyst is often the occasion for the release of emotion. Encouraging the patient to talk to this person, to mourn openly the loss of the significant other, results in an appropriate mourning and subsequent burial for the now psychologically ended relationship.

Some examples are less dramatic, yet more frequent in my day-by-day practice. A young man who had recently accepted a new position brought an initial dream in which he was driving his car up a hill. He looked at the gauges, saw that his engine was overheating, and felt that it might explode. He said that he did not think much of the dream, but it did scare him and so he thought I might want to see it.

I suggested that if we spent some time on it perhaps he could begin to see its relevance for him, and I simply reinforced his uneasy feeling about the dream. I suggested, after gathering personal associations to the dream, that it was as though he were in danger in his upward climb, and I asked him if aspects of his present life might not be a bit overwhelming for him right now.

He began to feel his fear. The story of his present and past efforts to achieve began to unfold. He admitted that he felt scared if he was not climbing, yet was afraid of what might happen to him. By the end of the session some of the immediate danger had passed. It was some time, however, before he began to face the deeper fear that was driving him upward. He felt that he had been born unwanted; he had to justify his right to be here. The danger expressed in the condition of his car warned him this was no solution to his fear.

Very often the dream is explicit about the particular emotion needing release. The dreamer may dream that he is crying or is angry, feels sad, or is in pain. When the dream ego is experiencing the emotion, it indicates the possibility that the conscious ego may now be ready to experience the emotion. I usually proceed with that assumption, but the experience may not occur immediately. Just as what the patient talks about in the first session will often be experienced later in the transference, what we dream of now often becomes conscious at a later time. Having heard a dream where the dream ego is expressing sorrow, for example, the analyst often needs simply to ask about such a feeling and wait.

Sometimes patients are encouraged to continue working on a dream image between analytical hours. A patient who had considerable analytical exposure took an image of a 911 Porsche and between sessions wrote out a dialogue with me concerning this image. During the course of this dialogue, he experienced a considerable release of emotion. He wrote:

> For a second my mind went blank.
> "My mind's a blank," I said.
> "Let your mind be blank. Don't fight it. Let it be very blank like a white movie screen with nothing on it. Just let the blankness be and if you begin to see anything tell me what you see."
> I paused. A fantasy raced through my mind in an instant. I went over it. It didn't make sense. So I waited for something that did. He interrupted my waiting. "Did you see anything on the screen?"
> "Well, not really," I lied.
> "Not really!" he replied, accenting the "really."
> I knew I would have to tell him. Suddenly, I felt I wanted to tell him.
> I began shyly, like a child testing the water for the first time.
> "I saw myself getting into a brand new 911 Porsche with a beautiful Japanese woman."
> I glanced at him quickly. I was surprised. He seemed interested. He did not give any indication that this was foolish or unusual. In abbreviated form he repeated what I had said.
> "A Porsche and a beautiful Japanese woman."
> His simple matter-of-fact repetition of what I had seen made me feel better. It was as though through his voice the fantasy was brought into this world. It was as though he were

welcoming a stranger in out of the cold, and I felt a rush of gratitude for his attitude toward what I had seen. I began to feel it was OK.

"So you have such a car, and do you have such a woman?" he asked matter-of-factly.

"No," I quickly replied. "The car costs too much. And I don't recognize the woman. She's different than the woman I know."

"Okay, then, tell me more about a 911 Porsche."

"No," he corrected himself, "be this 911 Porsche, and tell me about yourself. Speak in the first person, say, "I'm a Porsche, I'm . . .""

He made it so explicit I could not think of any questions to ask about how to go about this.

I started slowly, just repeating what he said.

"I'm a Porsche, I'm . . ."

I stopped.

"I'm what color," he asked?

"I'm blue," and then I began to blurt it all out. "I'm fast. I'm exciting. I'm reliable. I'm solid, hand-welded. Yes, I'm solid. I'm powerful. I'm precise. I'm a Targa."

"A Targa?"

"Yes, part of my roof comes off. I can let the air, the sun blow in. I can have fun. I can follow curves in the road without losing control. I can climb the mountains. I can go long distances. I'm solid yet I'm capable of exploring the most forbidden paths. I can go anywhere. I'm a one-man car. I'm faithful to my owner. I believe in him. If he cares for me I will care for him. I will take him wherever he needs to go and its okay with me."

I stopped, breathless, my face warm with excitement. I felt an inner glow.

He leaned back, and smiled, a deep satisfied smile, chuckled a few times and said with his own excitement,

"That's quite a car!"

"Now what about this woman with you. A car like that needs a beautiful woman. What about her?"

I could see he was really with me. He wasn't going to explain all this to me. I had the feeling he was going to ride right with me, with her, and together we were going to enjoy the ride.

I told him so.

He said, "Yes, let's do that. What about her. Let her speak for herself."

Without hesitating, I began.

"I belong here with this young man. I am his mystery. I'm different than he is. I will go where he goes. I will talk with him. I will not leave him. I will accept him in his joy and in his sadness. I will climb to the mountains and down to the valleys with him. I belong next to him. I love him."

I began to cry and as I cried I began to sob again and again, "I need someone to believe in me, I need someone to believe in me."

And when I stopped sobbing he simply said to me, "She believes in you, doesn't she?"

I nodded my head. I knew she did.

Again the release of emotion occurred when the meaning carried by the dream image was discovered. The patient's need for a feeling acceptance of his own potential represented by the Porsche was touched in the dialogue. He began to understand how much he needed to believe in himself, and the release of emotion began that process.

These examples underline the importance of valuing the particularity of each dream image. This provides the best guide regarding degree of emotion to be experienced, and the nature of the therapist's interventions.

There are many dream images, far too numerous to include here, that typically alert the therapist to the presence in the patient of strong emotion and its potentiality for release. A few more typically occurring images are: sudden fires, such as a house on fire; explosions or potential explosions, such as bombs bursting or a boiler overheating; images of flooding, such as rivers going over their banks, waves increasing in force, continuous rain; and images of uncontrolled power, fallen power lines, circuits sparking, images of natural disaster, wind storms, rain storms, forest fires. Experience with a wide range of such imagery sensitizes the therapist to the potentiality for emotional release revealed in the dream or in other unconscious symbolic expressions.

With each dream image, as illustrated in the previous examples, I attempt to provide a bridge to consciousness. I do this by analogy to whatever meaning or emotion I understand to be inhering in the dream image. I attempt to provide an analogy, crossing the chasm between my patient's ego and the dream message. I use the term "analogy" broadly to include my interpretations as, for example, when a simple comment about the negative qualities of the rat was offered. Sometimes the analogy is a parallel feeling —for example, when I simply reinforced the young man's fear of his upward climb. The Porsche example illustrates how the unconscious itself provided analogical meanings for the image of the car and woman.

In addition to supplying interpretation and feelings relevant to the meaning and emotion in the dream, I provide other analogies such as stories—personal, mythological, and religious. I may share a parallel fantasy. I may during the session show a patient a picture in a book similar to a dream image or painting that he has brought to the session. I may refer to a contemporary novel, movie, or selection of poetry. These analogies, the gathering and study of which is often a puzzle to other schools of thought, provide objective parallel meaning and emotion to the dream of the patient, enabling the patient's ego to connect with his unconscious, bringing back varying degrees of emotion and meaning.

Perhaps the clearest way to state a Jungian approach to the emotion-laden dream image would be through a fantasy: In relationship to the dream I see myself a fisherman, the fish representing a psychic content from the depths with both meaning and emotion. I study carefully the stream. I prefer to fish at dusk. I fish from the shadows and into the shadows of the stream. I am often alone on the stream. I catch a few small fish each day. Each one I hook and play differently, keeping myself sensitive to the particularity of this fish. I have tied my own flies, some are better than others, and when I begin fishing I try to determine, often intuitively, what fly I will use. I allow the fish to land itself. My hooks are small, but sharp.

REFERENCES

Chapter 1

Breuer, J. and Freud, S. 1955. *The standard edition of the complete psychological works of Sigmund Freud. Studies on Hysteria*, vol. 2. London: Hogarth Press.

Ellenberger, H. F. 1970. *The discovery of the unconscious.* New York: Basic Books.

Foucault, M. 1965. *Madness and civilization.* New York: Random House.

Janov, A. 1970. *The primal scream.* New York: Putnam.

Kiev, A. 1966. Prescientific psychiatry. In *American handbook of psychiatry*, vol. 3, ed. S. Arieti, p. 166–79. New York: Basic Books.

Mann, W. E. 1973. *Orgone, Reich and eros.* New York: Farrar, Straus and Giroux.

Perls, F. S. 1969. *Gestalt therapy verbatim.* Lafayette, Cal.: Real People Press.

Reich, W. 1970*a. Character analysis.* New York: Farrar, Straus and Giroux.

———. 1970*b. Listen, little man.* New York: Farrar, Straus and Giroux.

Rycroft, C. 1968. *A critical dictionary of psychoanalysis.* New York: Basic Books.

Chapter 2

Binswanger, L. 1963. *Being-in-the-world.* New York: Basic Books.

Boss, M. 1963. *Psychoanalysis and daseinsanalysis.* New York: Basic Books.

May, R. 1958. *Existence.* New York: Basic Books.

————. 1961. The context of psychotherapy. In *Contemporary psychothera-pies*, ed. Morris I. Stein. New York: Free Press of Glencoe.

Perls, F., Hefferline, R. F., and Goodman, P. 1951. *Gestalt therapy.* New York: The Julian Press.

Sartre, Jean-Paul. 1956. *Being and nothingness.* New York: Philosophical Library.

Chapter 4

Boudewyns, P. A., and Wilson, A. E. 1972. Implosive therapy and desensitization therapy using free association in the treatment of inpatients. *Journal of Abnormal Psychology* 79: 259–268.

Boulougouris, J. C.; Marks, I. M.; and Marset, P. 1971. Superiority of flooding (implosion) to desensitization for reducing pathological fears. *Behavior Research and Therapy* 9: 7–16.

Dollard, J., and Miller, N. E. 1950. *Personality and psychotherapy.* New York: McGraw-Hill.

Hogan, R. A. 1966. Implosive therapy in the short term treatment of psychotics. *Psychotherapy: Theory, Research, and Practice* 3: 25–32.

Levis, D. J. 1967. Implosive therapy, Part II: The subhuman analogue, the strategy, and the technique. *Behavioral modification techniques in the treatment of emotional disorders*, ed. S. G. Armitage, pp. 22–37. Battle Creek: V. A. Publications.

Levis, D. J., and Carrera, R. N. 1967. Effects of ten hours of implosive therapy in the treatment of outpatients. *Journal of Abnormal Psychology* 72: 504–508.

London, P. 1964. Teaching fearless behavior: the implosive therapy of Thomas G. Stampfl. In *The modes and morals of psychotherapy*, ed. P. London, pp. 95–109. New York: Holt, Rinehart & Winston.

Mowrer, O. H. 1939. A stimulus-response analysis of anxiety and its role as a reinforcing agent. *Psychological Review* 46: 553–565.

————. 1947. On the dual nature of learning—a reinterpretation of "conditioning" and "problem solving." *Harvard Educational Review* 17: 102–148.

————. 1956. Two-factor learning theory reconsidered, with special reference to secondary reinforcement and the concept of habit. *Psychological Review* 63: 114–128.

————. 1960a. *Learning theory and the symbolic processes.* New York: Wiley.

————. 1960b. *Learning theory and behavior.* New York: Wiley.

Ollendick, T. H., and Gruen, G. E. 1972. Treatment of a bodily injury phobia with implosive therapy. *Journal of Consulting and Clinical Psychology* 38: 389–393.

Rychlak, J. 1973. *Introduction to personality and psychotherapy.* Boston: Houghton Mifflin.

Shoben, E. J. 1949. Psychotherapy as a problem in learning theory. *Psychological Bulletin* 46: 366–392.

Smith, R. E., and Sharpe, T. M. 1970. Treatment of a school phobia with implosive therapy. *Journal of Consulting and Clinical Psychology* 35: 239–243.

Stampfl, T. G. 1967. Implosive therapy: The theory, the subhuman analogue, the strategy, and the technique. In *Behavioral modification techniques in the treatment of emotional disorders,* ed. S. G. Armitage, pp. 12–21. Battle Creek: V. A. Publications.

———. 1970. Implosive therapy: An emphasis on covert stimulation. In *Learning approaches to therapeutic behavior change,* ed. D. J. Levis, pp. 182–207. Chicago: Aldine Publishing.

Stampfl, T. G., and Levis, D. J. 1967. Essentials of implosive therapy: A learning-theory based psychodynamic behavioral therapy. *Journal of Abnormal Psychology* 6: 496–503.

———. 1967. Phobic patients: Treatment with the learning theory approach of implosive therapy. *Voices* fall: 23–27.

———. 1968. Implosive therapy: A behavior therapy? *Behavior Research and Therapy* 6: 31–36.

———. 1969. Learning theory: An aid to dynamic therapeutic practice. In *The relation of theory to practice in psychotherapy,* ed. L. D. Eron and R. Callahan, pp. 85–114. Chicago: Aldine Publishing.

Chapter 5

Fairbairn, W. R. D. 1952. *An object-relations theory of the personality.* New York: Basic Books.

Guntrip, H. 1964. *Personality structure and human interaction.* New York: International Universities Press.

———. 1968. *Schizoid phenomena, object relations and the self.* New York: International Universities Press.

Janov, A. 1970. *The primal scream.* New York: Putnam.

Chapter 6

Ament, P., and Milgrom, Halina. 1967. Effects of suggestion on pruritus with cutaneous lesions in chronic myelogenous leukemia. *New York State Journal of Medicine* 67: 833–835.

Black, S., and Friedman, M. 1968. Effects of emotion and pain on adrenocortical function investigated by hypnosis. *British Medical Journal* 1: 477–481.

Black, S., and Walter, W. G. 1965. Effects on anterior brain responses of variation in the probability of association between stimuli. *Journal of Psychosomatic Research* 9: 33–43.

Black, S., and Wigan, E. R. 1961. An investigation of selective deafness produced by direct suggestion under hypnosis. *British Medical Journal* 2: 736–741.

Gellhorn, E., and Loofbourrow, G. N. 1963. *Emotions and emotional disorders*. New York: Hoeber.

Horowitz, M. J. 1968. Visual images in psychotherapy. *American Journal of Psychotherapy* 22: 55–59.

Kline, M. V. 1952*a*. An outline of the nature of some sexual reactions to the induction of hypnosis. *Psychiatric Quarterly Supplement* 26: 230–236.

———. 1952*b*. Visual imagery and a case of experimental hypnotherapy. *Journal of Genetic Psychology* 46: 159–167.

———. 1953*a*. Hypnotic retrogression: A neuropsychological theory of age regression and progression. *Journal of Clinical and Experimental Hypnosis* 1: 21–28.

———. 1953*b*. Delimited hypnotherapy: The acceptance of resistance in the treatment of a long standing neurodermatitis with a sensory-imagery technique. *Journal of Clinical and Experimental Hypnosis* 1: 18-22.

———. 1953*c*. A visual imagery technique for the induction of hypnosis in certain refractory subjects. *Journal of Psychology* 35: 227–228.

———. 1954. Stimulus transformation and learning theory in the production and treatment of an acute attack of benign paroxysmal peritonitis. *Journal of Clinical and Experimental Hypnosis,* 1: 93–98.

———. 1960. Sensory-imagery techniques in hypnotherapy: Psychosomatic considerations. *Topical Problems in Psychotherapy* 3: 161–173.

———. 1963. Age regression and regressive procedures in hypnotherapy. In *Clinical correlations of experimental hypnosis,* ed. M. V. Kline, pp. 43–74. Springfield, Ill.: Thomas.

———. 1965. Hypnotherapy. In *The handbook of clinical psychology,* ed. B. Wolman. New York: McGraw-Hill.

———. 1966. Sensory hypnoanalysis. Paper presented at the 18th annual meeting, Society for Clinical and Experimental Hypnosis, New York.

————. 1967. Imagery, affect, and perception in hypnotherapy. In Psychodynamics and hypnosis: *New contributions to the practice and theory of hypnotherapy,* ed. M. V. Kline, pp. 41–70. Springfield, Ill.: Thomas.

Kline, M. V., and Linder, M. 1969. Psychodynamic factors in the experimental investigation of hypnotically induced emotions with particular reference to blood glucose measurements. *Journal of Psychology* 71: 21–25.

Maiolo, A. T.; Porro, B. G.; and Grannone, F. 1969. Cerebral haemodynamics and metabolism in hypnosis. *British Medical Journal* 1: 314.

Meares, A. 1960. *Shapes of sanity: A study in the therapeutic use of modelling in the waking and hypnotic state.* Springfield, Ill.: Thomas.

O'Connell, D., and Orne, M. T. 1968. Endosomatic electrodermal correlates of hypnotic depth and susceptibility. *Journal of Psychiatric Research* 6: 1–12.

Raginsky, B. B. 1962. Sensory hypnoplasty with case illustrations. *International Journal of Clinical and Experimental Hypnosis* 10: 205–219.

————. 1967. Rapid regression to oral and anal levels through sensory hypnoplasty. In *Hypnosis and psychosomatic medicine: Proceedings of the International Congress for Hypnosis and Psychosomatic Medicine,* ed. J. Lassner, pp. 253–263. New York: Springer-Verlag.

Sargent, W. 1957. *Battle for the Mind.* London: Heinemann.

Schneck, J. M. 1950. Psychosomatic reactions to the induction of hypnosis. *Dis. Nervous System* 11: 118–121.

————. 1952. The elucidation of spontaneous sensory and motor phenomena during hypnoanalysis. *Psychoanalytic Review* 39: 79–89.

Shorvon, H. J., and Sargent, W. 1947. Excitatory abreaction. *Journal of Mental Science* 93: 709–732.

Weller, C.; Linder, M.; Nuland, W.; and Kline, M. V. 1961. The effects of hypnotically induced emotions on continuous, uninterrupted blood glucose measurements. *Psychosomatic Medicine* 5: 38.

Chapter 8

Lowen, A. 1971. What is bioenergetic analysis. *Energy and Character.* 2, No. 3: 5–7.

Chapter 10

Abraham, K. 1956 (1911). Note on the psychoanalytic investigation and treatment of manic depressive insanity and allied conditions. In

Selected papers, pp. 137–156. London: Institute of Psychoanalysis and Hogarth Press.

Bak, R. C. 1953. Fetishism. *Journal of the American Psychoanalytic Association* 1: 285–298.

Bowlby, J., and Parks, C. M. 1970. Separation and loss within the family. In *The child in his family,* vol. 1, eds. E. J. Anthony and C. Koupirnik, pp. 197–216. New York: Wiley.

Engel, G. L. 1961. Is grief a disease? A challenge for medical research. *Psychosomatic Medicine* 23: 18–22.

Fenichel, O. 1945. *The psychoanalytic theory of neurosis.* New York: Norton.

Fintzy, R. T. 1971. Vicissitudes of the transitional object in a borderline child. *International Journal of Psycho-analysis* 52: 107–114

Freud, S. 1957a. (1917). *Mourning and melancholia.* In *Standard edition of the complete psychological works of Sigmund Freud,* vol. 14, ed. J. Strachey, pp. 237–260. London: Hogarth Press.

———. 1957b. (1938). Splitting of the ego in the process of defense. In *Standard edition,* vol. 23, pp. 275–278.

Greenacre, P. 1969. The fetish and the transitional object. *The psychoanalytic study of the child,* vol. 24, pp. 144–164. New York: International Universities Press.

———. 1970. The transitional object and the fetish with special reference to the role of illusion. *International Journal of Psycho-analysis* 51: 447–456.

Kübler-Ross, E. 1969. *On death and dying.* New York: Macmillan.

Mahler, M. S. 1968 *On human symbiosis and the vicissitudes of individuation,* vol. 1. New York: International Universities Press.

Modell, A. H. 1970. The transitional objects and the creative art. *Psychoanalytic Quarterly,* 39: 240–250.

Pollock, G. 1961. Mourning and adaptation. *International Journal of Psycho-analysis* 42: 341–361.

Rado, S. 1956. Adaptational development of psychoanalytic therapy. In *Changing concepts of psychoanalytic medicine,* eds. S. Rado and G. E. Daniels, pp. 89–100. New York: Grune and Stratton.

Schofield, W. 1966. The structured personality inventory in measurement of effects of psychotherapy. In *Methods of research in psychotherapy,* eds. L. A. Gottschalk and A. H. Auerback, pp. 536–550. New York: Appleton-Century-Crofts.

Volkan, V. D. 1966. Normal and pathological grief reactions—a guide for the family physician. *Virginia Medical Monthly* 93: 651–656

———. 1970. Typical findings in pathological grief. *Psychiatric Quarterly,* 44: 231–250.

————. 1971. A study of a patient's re-grief work through dreams, psychological tests and psychoanalysis. *Psychiatric Quarterly* 45: 255–273.

————. 1972*a*. The recognition and prevention of pathological grief. *Virginia Medical Monthly* 99: 535–540.

————. 1972*b*. The linking objects of pathological mourners. *Archives of General Psychiatry* 27: 215–221.

————. 1973. Transitional fantasies in the analysis of a narcissistic personality. *Journal of the American Psychoanalytic Association* 21: 351–376.

————. 1974. Death, divorce and the physician. In *Marital and sexual counseling in medical practice,* eds. D. W. Abse, L. M. Nash, and L. M. R. Louden, pp. 446–462. New York: Harper and Row.

————. In press. More on linking objects. In *Bereavement,* ed. A. H. Kutscher. New York: Columbia University Press.

Volkan, V. D., and Showalter, C. R. 1968. Known object loss, disturbance in reality testing, and "re-grief" work as a method of brief psychotherapy. *Psychiatric Quarterly* 42: 358–374.

Winnicott, D. W. 1953. Transitional objects and transitional phenomena. *International Journal of Psycho-analysis* 34: 89–97.

Chapter 11

Assagioli, R. 1965. *Psychosynthesis: A manual of principles and techniques.* New York: Hobbs, Dorman.

Malamud, D. 1973*a*. Self-confrontation methods in psychotherapy. *Psychotherapy: Theory, Research and Practice* 10: 123–130.

————. 1973*b*. The god exercise: A self-confrontation technique. *Voices* 9: 24–28.

Perls, F. S. 1969. *Gestalt therapy verbatim.* Lafayette, Cal.: Real People Press.

SUBJECT INDEX

Parent(s)
  relationships with, and awareness of
    self, 237
  surrogate, therapist as, 92
Patient(s)
  important role in therapy, 137
  selection of, for re-grief therapy,
    189-191
  types of, in intense feeling therapy,
    89-90
Pavlov, Ivan Petrovich, transmarginal
    inhibition of, 113
Pelvic armor, 18
Pelvis
  importance in Structural Integration,
    132, 134
  as last defense, 18
Perceptual functions, and ground-
    ing, 145
Periotonitis, benign paroxysmal,
    hypnotherapy in, 97
Perls, Frederick S., and Gestalt therapy,
    25, 31-32
Personality traits, of pathological
    mourner, 190-191
Phenomenological observation, in
    Gestalt therapy, 31-32, 35
Photographs, use in re-grief therapy,
    197, 205-206, 207, 213, 214, 216
Physiological function, integrated, 135
Plasticine modeling, in sensory hypno-
    plasty, 98, 99
Polygraphic monitoring, in hypnosis,
    116, 121-123
Possession, demonic, as diagnostic
    category, 13
Pre-oedipal stage, vs. oedipal stage, as
    focus of therapy, 92
Presence
  as essential to encounter, 26, 27
  use of term, 29
Primal community, need for, 90
Primaling, 81
  in intense feeling therapy, 88-89
The Primal Scream (Janov), 80
Primals, in intense feeling therapy,
    86-88

Primal therapy, 19
  post-primal patients, 93
  See also Intense feeling therapy
Primitive cures, linked to modern tech-
    niques, 12
Primitive societies, and use of flooding
    techniques, 11-12
Projection, 34
Projective psychological testing, and
    sensory hypnoanalysis, 103
Protagonist
  defined, 40
  and resistance in psychodrama, 55
  and silencing signal, 50
Protest phase, of loss-grieving cycle,
    152
Provocative maneuvers, of therapists, 19
Psoriasis, hypnotherapy in, 97
Psychoanalysis
  and change in techniques, 16
  use of emotional drought, 137
Psychoanalytic schools, and emotion,
    80
Psychodrama
  example of, 44-46
  integrating feeling with insight, 166
  procedure, 43-44
  techniques of, glossary of terms, 40
Psychosomatic medicine, practiced by
    shamans, 12
Psychosomatic symptoms, and sensory
    hypnoanalysis, 100, 112
Psychotherapeutics, nineteenth-century,
    15
Psychotherapy, waking, combined with
    hypnoanalysis, 101

Rats, symbolism of, 244
Reality
  relation to encounter, and trans-
    ference, 28
  and self-awareness, 37
Redintegration, in implosive therapy, 62
Regression
  as "death primal," 90
  in intense feeling therapy, 81, 95
  in pathological mourning, 189

265

267

NAME INDEX

Abraham, K., 183, 255
Ament, P., 98, 253
Asher, Charles W., 7, 239
Assagioli, R., 226, 257
Badin, Irwin, 83
Bak, R. C., 223, 256
Bellis, John M., 7, 136
Binswanger, L., 26, 251
Black, Abraham, 72
Black, S., 115, 254
Boss, Medard, 26-27, 251
Boudewyns, Patrick, 76, 252
Boulougouris, J. C., 76, 252
Bowlby, John, 152, 181, 256
Breuer, J., 15, 251
Brown, Judson, 72
Brush, Robert, 72
Buber, Martin, 26
Carlson, James, 72
Carrera, Richard, 76
Church, Russel, 72
Cilluffo, Anthony F., 9, 179, 190
Denes-Radomisli, Magda, 7, 25
Denny, Ray, 72
Dollard, J., 71, 252
Ellenberger, Henri, 12, 15, 251
Engel, G. L., 180, 256
Fairburn, W. R. D., 92, 253
Fenichel, O., 184, 256
Fintzy, R. T., 221, 256
Foucault, M., 14-15, 251
Freud, Sigmund, 15, 80-81, 91-92,
     143, 181, 183, 251, 256
Friedman, M., 115, 254

Gelhorn, E., 113, 116, 254
Goldstein, Kurt, 25
Golias, George, 76
Goodman, P., 32, 252
Grannone, F., 115, 255
Greenacre, P., 221, 256
Gruen, G. E., 252
Gumina, James, 76
Guntrip, H., 92, 253
Hefferline, R. F., 32, 252
Hogan, Robert, 76, 252
Horowitz, M. J., 115, 254
Janov, A., 80, 91, 93, 251, 253
Kalish, Harold, 72
Kamin, Leon, 72
Keleman, Stanley, 167, 169
Keyes, Margaret Frings, 8, 151
Kiev, A., 12, 251
Kline, Milton V., 8, 96, 97, 98, 99,
     101, 114, 254, 255
Kübler-Ross, E., 180, 256
Lamers, William M., Jr., 152
Levis, Donald, 76, 252, 253
Linder, M., 255
London, P., 252
Loofburrow, G. N., 113, 116, 254
Lowen, Alexander, 138, 143, 146,
     167, 255
McAllister, 72
Mahler, M.S., 187, 256
Maiolo, A. T., 115, 255
Malamud, Daniel I., 8, 225, 226, 257
Mann, W. E., 17, 18, 251
Marks, I. M., 76, 252

269